More weirdness on the Web?
YOU'D BETTER BELIEVE IT!

Crave even more of the zany, strange, and unbelievable?
Visit our top-secret website, **www.ripleys.com/members**,
where you'll find tons of **BRAND NEW, WEB-ONLY** downloadable activities:

• Crazy crafts you can print out and make •
• Cool coloring pages of some of our wildest Ripley's items •
• Wacky screen savers to decorate your desktop •
And MORE!

All of our weird, wild, and wonderful Ripley's books are also available online!
Visit our website, www.ripleys.com/books!

PUBLISHING

Publishing Director Anne Marshall
Editorial Director Becky Miles
Art Director Sam South
Senior Designer Michelle Foster
Assistant Editor Charlotte Howell
Design Ark Creative
Reprographics Juice Creative

For information regarding permission, write to: VP Intellectual Property,
Ripley Entertainment Inc.,
Suite 188, 7576 Kingspointe Parkway, Orlando, Florida 32819, USA
email: publishing@ripleys.com

ISBN 978-1-60991-129-4

10 9 8 7 6 5 4 3 2 1

Printed in China
In January 2015
1st printing

Ripley's—
Believe It or Not!®

YIKES!

FANTASTIC FEATS, STORIES, FUN, AND FACTS

Illustrated by John Graziano

YiKES!

feats

You won't believe the crazy things people do when you look inside this fun-packed book! Meet the man who runs backward, the woman who lived with scorpions, and the man who can pull a schoolbus, plus many more! **It's Ripley's Shout Outs!**

INTRODUCING... JOHN GRAZIANO

John, Ripley's very own cartoonist, has drawn every cartoon in this wacky book of crazy things people do.

A new Ripley's cartoon has been produced every day for the past 90 years by a dedicated Ripley's cartoonist. John is only the eighth person to take on this role. Amazingly, he got himself the job 25 years after sending his drawings to Ripley's as a teenager!

SPEEDY QUESTIONS!

1. Q: What tools do you use for your drawings?
A: My actual drawings are done the old-fashioned way: with pencil, pen and ink, and brush and ink to paper. For airbrushing and coloring, I use a Wacom digital tablet.

2. Q: If you hadn't become an artist what would you be?
A: I actually wanted to be a paleontologist and dig up fossils! I do that as a hobby though.

3. Q: Which story in Yikes! do you think is the wackiest?
A: Definitely "Extreme Ironing"!

4. Q: Which of the crazy feats would you try yourself?
A: I'd love to be inside Fan Yang's enormous bubble, and then pop it!

BABY BOAT

Hugo Vihlen from Florida has sailed the seas in a boat the size of a bathtub. He made his first Atlantic crossing in 1968 in a sailboat measuring only 5 feet 11 inches. It took him 84 days and he traveled

4,100 MILES

facing huge waves and strong winds. Then, in 1993 Englishman Tom McNally set sail in an even smaller boat, measuring a tiny 5 feet 4½ inches. Hugo then proceeded to saw down his boat until it measured the smaller size of 5 feet 4 inches—and crossed from Canada to England in 115 days.

Need a big cuddle? In 2008, 12,000 students in Ottawa, Ontario, Canada, all hugged each other at the same time.

Have you ever tried it? C. Manoharan certainly has. He swallowed 200 live earthworms, all of them at least 4 inches long, in just 20 seconds in November 2003. Eeoogh!

SHOOTING STAR

1 David "Cannonball" Smith has performed his human cannonball circus act for 30 years.

2 The audience watch as he prepares to enter the cannon.

3 He awaits ignition and is fired out at great speed with a loud bang!

4 BOOM!

In 1998, his speed was recorded as 70 mph, and he traveled over 185 feet through the air.

11

UP, UP, AND AWAY

Have you ever held a helium balloon and wondered if a few more would lift you into the sky? That's exactly what Kent Couch decided to try, and in 2008 he actually did it. He flew nearly 235 miles across Oregon using a lawn chair with over 100 large balloons tied to it. His flying machine took him up through the clouds, reaching a top speed of 49 mph. He landed safely by popping the balloons.

Babu Chhiri Sherpa is the only person to have slept at the top of Mount Everest, the world's highest mountain. He spent over 21 hours at the summit in 1999.

Come back!

Most marathon runners are wiped out after their event, but not U.S. runner Dane Rauschenberg. The 30-year-old soon found that he can just keep on running, and set up his Fiddy 2 (fifty-two) charity event in which he ran a full 26.2-mile marathon every weekend, for a whole year.

FACE THE MUSIC

Can you play an instrument? Can you whistle? Maybe you can... but can you play bells with your eyebrows? F.G. Holt of Nashville, Arkansas, could play popular tunes with bells attached to his eyebrows, to show how well he could control his facial muscles.

13

KEEP TRYING...

Back to front

Can you twist your head half a circle to see behind you? If you can, you can join the Bird Men of Guinea, a secret society of African acrobats!

Watery world

Turkish diver Cem Karabay submerged himself in a tank full of water outside a shopping mall in Istanbul, Turkey, and stayed there for 5½ days. The tank measured 16 feet by 10 feet by 10 feet and Cem was on view eating, drinking, exercising, and sleeping for the whole 135 hours. While in the tank, he suffered with high blood pressure and an eye infection, yet he still wants to do it again!

WOW!

AWESOME!

That's amazing

"Human flag" Dominic Lacasse from Canada is so strong he can hold himself stretched horizontally on a bar, just like a flag, for 39 seconds.

UHHHH!

Hanging around

Greg Gasson is one of the world's best stunt skydivers, and he trains and plans his stunts to the smallest degree. For one stunt he leaped out of the plane and then held on to his parachute with one hand! He hung like that above Eloy, Arizona, thousands of feet in the air, but then climbed back into the main parachute harness to land safely.

HMS popsicle

In 2008, Robert McDonald set sail on a boat made from 15 million popsicle sticks from the Netherlands to England. It took Robert, from Emmeloord, Holland, four years to build with the help of 5,000 school kids.

In April 2009, pensioner Les Pugh abseiled 160 feet down the side of an office block in Cheltenham, England. Les dressed in smart jacket, shirt and tie, was 93 years old!

Cube dude

Leyan Lo from California can solve a Rubik's cube in less than 1 hour and 30 minutes—blindfolded! Let him see it and he can do it in an amazing 11.13 seconds.

CROSSED WORDS

Abdul-Karim Qasem from the Yemen has created the world's biggest crossword puzzle. It is 178 times bigger than any other crossword! It has

320,500 SQUARES

and a whole book of clues, and it took him seven years to make up. The clues contain 800,720 words and he researched each clue carefully so nothing in the puzzle is repeated.

Sting in the tale

Thailand's "Scorpion Queen" Kanchana Kaetkaew not only loves scorpions, she lives with them. In 2002 and again in 2008–9 she spent a month in a glass box, surrounded by between 3,000 and 5,000 live scorpions. They do sting her, but her body is so used to scorpion venom it seems to be immune to it. Kanchana feeds the super stingers and performs with them each day, including putting them in her mouth.

YIKES!

Stilt walking is a tricky talent to master, but Jeff Jay has taken it to new heights: 60 feet, in fact. He created the giant stilts himself and has to be lifted on to them by a crane!

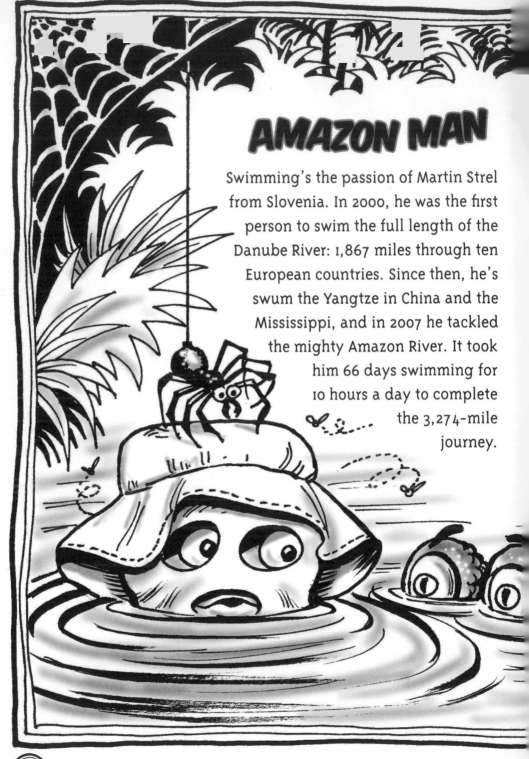

AMAZON MAN

Swimming's the passion of Martin Strel from Slovenia. In 2000, he was the first person to swim the full length of the Danube River: 1,867 miles through ten European countries. Since then, he's swum the Yangtze in China and the Mississippi, and in 2007 he tackled the mighty Amazon River. It took him 66 days swimming for 10 hours a day to complete the 3,274-mile journey.

YIKES!

He had to wear a protective suit against piranhas, snakes, spiders, and parasitic fish, and have armed guards in a boat next to him to fire at pirates. That's not to mention needing to fight off any attacks from crocodiles and sharks.

HELP!

Holy rolling

The "Rolling Saint" of India, real name Lotan Baba, has rolled nearly

19,000 MILES

between towns and cities, spreading a message of peace to all he meets. He rolls his body along the ground and covers up to

8 MILES A DAY!

It's a change from the seven years he spent standing upright in the same spot under a banyan tree.

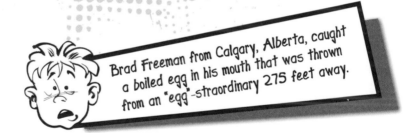

Brad Freeman from Calgary, Alberta, caught a boiled egg in his mouth that was thrown from an "egg"-straordinary 275 feet away.

Ear ache

Have you ever tried a tug-of-war using your ear to pull the string? That's what happens in Arctic North America. The Inuit people compete by placing the looped end of the string on one ear, and pulling steadily backward to see who can win.

FEARLESS FEELINE

Don't call the fire service to rescue this cat: It's part of a special performance. Hopefully, the poor puss isn't "pet"-rified while perched in a basket on top of a ladder,

24 FEET

in the air. To make the act even more amazing, Bob Dotzauer of Cedar Rapids, Iowa, balances the ladder on his chin!

Ripley's HEAD STRONG

Brilliant balancer John Evans from Wales can hold aloft all sorts of objects—and he balances them on his head. That might sound easy, but he tackles some heavy stuff, such as pieces of wooden furniture weighing more than an adult!

He's lifted 84 milk crates together... and two women on his head at the same time.

And finally: 92 people, one after the other, for an amazing 10 seconds each!

John held a car on his head for 2 minutes.

Fourteen-year-old Akash Gupta played the guitar for 53 hours (over 2 days), non-stop, in Agra, India, in June 2008.

Pair up

If you can't find your socks one morning, blame the people working at the Tripsdill Amusement Park in Cleebronn, Germany. Staff there have hung up over

20,000 SOCKS

to make a washing line that is 7,553 feet long: Nearly a mile and a half! They don't actually steal the socks, but they do ask visitors if they will donate a pair to add to the line.

Fire hazard

Record-breaker Ashrita Furman took part in a huge birthday celebration on August 27, 2005. Altogether, 50 people were needed to light the 27,413 candles on a birthday cake that measured 47 feet by 3 feet. The cake was to celebrate the birthday of the Sri Chinmoy Centre in New York City.

Norwegian explorer Boerge Ousland was the first person to travel solo across Antarctica. He took 64 days with no one there to help him on his trek.

Ready, steady, crawl!

Even babies can be sporty… in 2006, the city of Cali in California held a special crawling race! Tiny tots from eight to 18 months were invited to take part and crawl along a track that was 16 feet long. More than 1,100 keep-fit crawlers joined in, and the winner received a special bag full of baby booty.

In 1987, UK muscleman Garry Windebank held up 101 tires weighing nearly 1,500 pounds.

Flight fright

Mark Malkoff from New York was so scared of flying that he took on an unusual challenge to get over it. He agreed to spend a whole month on an airplane, and wasn't even allowed to enter an airport, so he had to shower and sleep on the plane or at the runway. By the end of the month he had flown on

135 FLIGHTS

landed at

38 U.S. RUNWAYS

and traveled over

100,000 MILES

(more than four times round the world).

Alexandra Nechita from Romania was only eight years old when she held her first painting exhibition at a Los Angeles library in 1993.

Driller thriller

Thomas Blackthorne from Cornwall, England, wowed audiences with his 2007 performance on a German TV show. During his dangerous act he swallowed the moving parts of a jackhammer—the kind of drill used for breaking concrete—and even had the drill turned on for five seconds. Although his life was at risk, all he actually suffered afterward was a sore mouth.

WOW!

Call collect

Squeeze in everyone! In 2003, 14 members of the Kabosh theater group from Belfast, Northern Ireland, squashed themselves into a single phone booth.

Jewgenij Kuschnow balanced on the roof of a moving car in Munich, Germany, in 2006 for 15 minutes—standing on his head!

Big surf

An enormous surfboard, measuring 40 feet long and 10 feet wide, was used on the Australian Gold Coast in 2005. It was big enough to fit 47 surfers, who stayed on for four minutes.

Head count

What's 75,634,981 x 53,672,008? What do you mean, you need a calculator? The 18th-century mathematician Johann Dase could work out sums like that in his head in less than a minute! He wasn't particularly clever, but was exceptionally good at mental calculations. He could also multiply two 20-digit numbers in six minutes, and was said to be able to tell how many sheep were in a field by looking at them, not counting.

Wobbly walk

Clifford Calverley, a tightrope walker from Toronto, Canada, walked over Niagara Falls in 1892. He balanced on a steel cable and took 6½ minutes to teeter across.

In February 2006, 3,745 people had an enormous snowball fight in Houghton, Michigan.

AWESOME!

Playing with fire

Yosuke Yamashita played a piano that was on fire! He wore a flame-retardant suit to protect his body as he improvised a jazz piece, but had to stop after 10 minutes when the flames burned through the piano strings.

27

Big breath

Famous magician David Blaine pushes himself to the limits for each of his performances. In May 2006, he spent 7 days and nights underwater in a "human aquarium." His final underwater challenge was to hold his breath for 9 minutes, while he freed his hands and feet from heavy chains—but after 7 minutes and 8 seconds, he had to be lifted out by divers.

Eeoogh! In 2002, Christine Martin from Horsham, England, spent an hour and a half in a bathtub full of maggots.

Hitching a ride

Kris Mole from Sussex, England, traveled around Europe with no money at all. He hitchhiked rides from motorists, accepted accommodation from strangers, and if no one offered food or a bed, he didn't eat or sleep. All he spent was time—six months to cover nearly 10,000 miles and visit 26 capital cities.

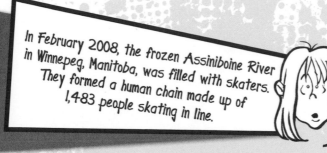

In February 2008, the frozen Assiniboine River in Winnepeg, Manitoba, was filled with skaters. They formed a human chain made up of 1,483 people skating in line.

COMING OR GOING?

Swiss runner Rinaldo Inabnit might look to be running away from you, but he's not: He just runs backward! He uses a

REARVIEW MIRROR

to see where he's going, and once ran backward up a mountain for 7 miles! He knows people think "retro-running" is a strange sport, but he likes to use his body in a different way from normal.

Ripley's
LIVING IN A BUBBLE

Some people can turn a balloon into a dog or a giraffe, but Lars Lottrup can turn a clown into a balloon! The Danish clown loves amazing his audiences with his favorite trick, during which he gradually gets himself sucked right inside a giant orange balloon.

1 Just clowning around.

2 Lars disappears headfirst...

3 ... oh, there he is!

Mad hatter

Gary Hatter has been all around the U.S.A. on a lawn mower! He started his mower marathon in Portland, Maine, in May 2000 and arrived at Daytona Beach, Florida, in February 2001. During his travels he visited all 48 mainland states, and Canada and Mexico, and covered nearly 15,000 miles.

OH, BEE QUIET!

Dr. Norman Gary gets a buzz from jazz... and from bees. The Professor of Entomology (insect studies) at the University of California takes his Thriller Bee Show all around the world. In the show, he shuts himself in a box with around 100,000 bees and plays his clarinet. The bees even buzz into his mouth while he plays, and he does get stung, but it doesn't seem to send him out of tune!

Juergen Koehler is the fastest man on inline skates. The German breaks speed records by holding on to a Porsche traveling at 180 mph.

Don't try this at home

Marco Boehm appeared on a German TV show in 2007 and showed the viewers an unusual way to stop an electric fan from whizzing round—he stopped it with his tongue! Surely it's much safer to turn it off at the switch?

Frenchman Marco Siffredi snowboarded his way down the world's highest mountain, Mount Everest, in 2001.

CORN MAD!

Do you like popcorn? Not as much as Crazy Legs Conti, maybe, who was buried alive in the stuff and had to eat his way out. Standing in a glass box he was totally covered in buttered popcorn, and had to breathe through a snorkel until he'd eaten past neck level. He had colored lights to show how he was doing: Red meant "danger," green "all's okay," and yellow "bring more butter!"

ON THE EDGE...

Walk all over
Dave Kunst from Caledonia, Minnesota, has walked around the world! He took 1,568 days, wore out 21 pairs of shoes, and covered 14,450 miles—that's more than 20 million steps.

Living the sky life
Felix Baumgartner from Austria is a seriously scary skydiver. On July 31, 2003, he launched himself from a plane at 30,000 feet, and crossed the English Channel in freefall. His only equipment was an oxygen tank, a parachute, and a carbon-fiber wing measuring 6 feet across. He glided the 22-mile channel crossing in just 14 minutes and then opened his parachute to land in Calais, France.

WILD!

AMAZING!

Lighting the way
Feeling flash? Harry Rifas certainly was. The former paratrooper from Bronx, New York City, could swallow and then regurgitate seven flashlight bulbs.

Days are numbered

Les Stewart of Mudjimba, Australia, typed out every number up to a million, in words, and printed them out, using nearly 20,000 pieces of paper. Typing for 20 minutes every hour, on the hour, it took him 15 years to complete. When asked why he did it, he said simply it was to give him something to do. He still has the first and last sheets, but has discarded all the rest.

> One, two, miss a few, nine-hundred-and-ninety nine-thousand-nine hundred-and-ninety nine... one million!

Top twosome

Acrobats Miguel and Rosa Vazquez had such high hopes for their future together that they got married in the middle of their act, on top of the high trapeze platform! The wedding took place in December 1983 at the Ringling Bros. and Barnum & Bailey Circus in Venice, Florida.

AWESOME!

Catch him if you can: Gary Stewart from Ohio jumped 177,737 times without falling off his pogo stick in May 1990. He was pogoing for 20 hours non-stop.

ZZZZZZZZZ

ROLL WITH IT

How would you like to walk through the big cat enclosure of a safari park? That's exactly what Arnd Drossel did in 2007—but he was in his own "cage." It was a huge steel mesh ball, much like a giant hamster ball, and Arnd walked 220 miles through Germany in it.

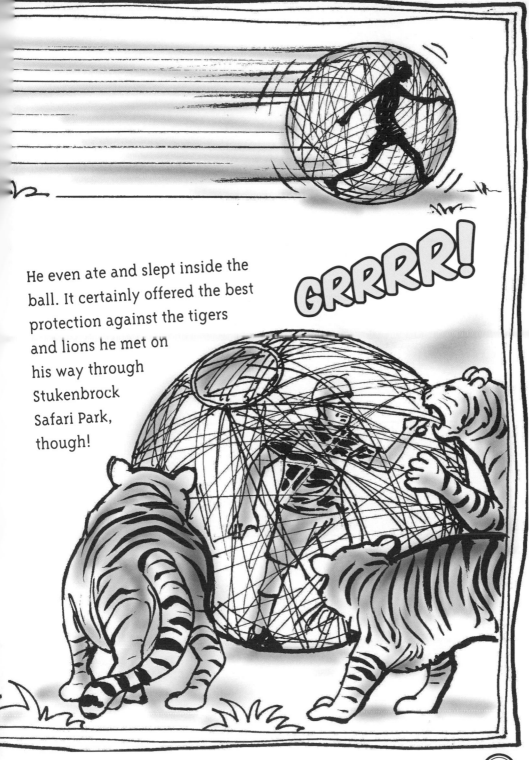

He even ate and slept inside the ball. It certainly offered the best protection against the tigers and lions he met on his way through Stukenbrock Safari Park, though!

GRRRR!

TRADING PLACE

Canadian Kyle MacDonald spent a year trading on the Internet, swapping items for bigger and better things each time. He began with a giant red paperclip, and ended up with a house!

Paperclip...

wooden fish pen...

doorknob...

camping stove to electric generator...

neon beer sign...

snowmobile...

It took just 14 trades, including a doorknob, a snowmobile and a ski vacation, and Kyle's last trade took him from a movie role to proud houseowner.

ski vacation to a van...

recording contract...

afternoon with Alice Cooper...

apartment for one year...

snow globe to movie role...

a house!

Bedtime reading?

The world's biggest atlas was unveiled at the 2010 Frankfurt Book Fair, Germany. Forget about reading under the covers—the book measures 6½ feet by nearly 10 feet and took three hours to move into position at the book fair! It costs $100,000 and is a 580-page atlas of the world, simply called *Earth*.

In 2000, Josh Tenge from Nevada carried out a back flip on his sandboard that was 44 feet 10 inches long!

Many marathons

In 2007, Canadian runner Richard Takata ran marathons in New Zealand, the U.S.A., Egypt, Spain, Antarctica, Argentina, and Cyprus. That's a mega-impressive marathon on each of the seven continents. What's more he ran them all in just under 30 days.

BUBBLE BONANZA

Fan Yang is forever blowing bubbles. He makes bubbles with bubbles inside, bouncing bubbles, colored bubbles, and chains of bubbles that float in the air. He can make bubbles so strong that people can step right into them. In 2004, in California, he fit 15 people inside a bubble. His longest bubble was a wall measuring 156 feet long!

CHEW-CHEW CHAIN

Canadian Gary Duschl has spent over 40 years making a chain from gum wrappers: Over one million of them! He started in 1965 with 20 wrappers, and the chain now stretches for 9 miles. It contains wrappers from more than

$50,000 - WORTH OF GUM

but Gary admits that even he couldn't chew that much by himself—lots of the wrappers are sent to him by fans who have heard about his chain challenge.

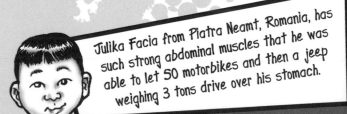

Julika Facia from Piatra Neamt, Romania, has such strong abdominal muscles that he was able to let 50 motorbikes and then a jeep weighing 3 tons drive over his stomach.

BACK ATCHA!

Barnaby Ruhe is a boomerang master. He can control one so well that when he throws it, it travels 100 feet and returns to hit an egg on top of his own head! Just occasionally he misthrows, and gets a whack on the nose, but he has "egg"-spertly thrown it over 100 times to zero in on the right target.

BMX BALANCE

Ever seen extreme yoga in action? Well, here you go:
It's Khiv Raj Gurjar from Rajasthan, India, who mixes his
love of bikes and yoga and takes to the mountain tops to
show off his moves. Khiv has practiced yoga for over
50 years, and can perform 36 different positions
on his BMX, 300 feet up a mountain.

Beat that

Cover your ears! In July 2009 at the National Indoor Arena in Birmingham, England, 582 drummers all drummed together for five minutes. They kept to the same rhythm at the same speed, which was apparently the easy part. Getting them all to stop at the same time was the real problem....

As part of a special challenge, 32,000 New Zealanders brushed their teeth at exactly 1.45 p.m. on August 7, 2006.

Piece of pi

The mathematical number pi, which relates to the measurements around and across a circle, is easiest to remember as 3.14. However, it actually has infinite (never ending) decimal places, and in 2005 Akira Haraguchi reeled off over 80,000 of them overnight! He started around noon and reached his previous best of 54,000 after dark. He stopped early the next day when he had recited 83,431 decimal places.

HIGH AND MIGHTY

Chinese hero Adhil, "King of the Sky," has no fear of heights. He is famous for his breathtaking high-wire acts, and in 2003 he walked along a narrow wire fixed 2,200 feet above Tiankeng Canyon. It took him an amazing 8 hours and 12 minutes.

Super-surfer Daniel Messier from Canada spent 4 days and 7 hours surfing the Internet without a break in 1997.

RIPLEY's
VERY LUCKY STRIKE

Bowling isn't easy at the best of times, but bowling backward makes life even more tricky! Jim Cripps, from Nashville, Tennessee, first tried it as a joke—and scored a strike. Then he practiced for weeks to win a bet and prove he could score 150 bowling in reverse. His best backward score is 279, with 11 consecutive strikes in one game!

Shoulder holder

Joe Jirgles from Grand Rapids, Michigan, was famous in the 1940s for his amazing shoulder strength. He could use his shoulder blades to attach himself to a fence and hang above the ground, and could even place a gallon can of varnish between his shoulder blades and keep it there.

Alexander Bendikov from Belarus balances matchsticks on bottles. Not so amazing—until you see him do it with 18,000 matches on a single bottleneck.

HARD PRESSED

Ironing can be pretty boring, so Phil Shaw from Leicester, England, decided to spice it up a little and created "extreme ironing." The first World Championships took place in 2002, and competitors had to iron in all sorts of places. Extreme ironers can smooth out the creases in their clothes just about anywhere: on mountains, underwater, surfing downriver,

Skydiving

In the Antarctic

Cycling

Hang-gliding

in an underground cavern, even while parachuting and hang-gliding!

Underwater

WAY TO GO...

Paper craft
In 1619, English poet and working water boatman John Taylor made a brown paper boat and sailed in it for 40 miles down the River Thames. In 2003, British comedian Tim FitzHigham blew that record out of the water by rowing 160 miles along the Thames for charity in a boat made of paper and glue. He mended it with sticky tape during the 8 days he was on the water.

An Indian barber named Jai Narain Bhati spent 108 hours in 2002 cutting hair. He managed to cut the hair of 1,451 people!

Boy wonder
When he was only two years old, Anthony McQuone from Weybridge, England, could quote lines from Shakespeare and speak Latin.

WOW!

Juggling time
Czech Republic juggling expert Zdenek Bradác is super speedy. In July 2009, he juggled three balls for 60 seconds, during which time he caught them 339 times.

Nippy dipper

Richard Rodriguez from Brooklyn, New York, just loves to ride roller coasters—so much so that he spent 17 days straight on them! He took the challenge at Blackpool Pleasure Beach, England, spending his days on the Pepsi Max Big One. He ate and drank on the ride, but had to switch to a smaller ride at night where he managed to grab 40 winks now and then.

Englishman Adrian Wigley played an organ non-stop for two hours using his tongue, not his fingers.

Air-raising

If you were given a balloon to blow up, chances are you'd put it to your lips and blow. Not so for Zhang Yingmin, from Shandong Province in China: He holds his nose, breathes in, and blows out through pipes to inflate the balloon with air coming from his ears and eyes!

Small call

How small is your cellphone? The smallest telephone in the world was built in 1996 by Jan Krutewicz from Munster, Illinois, and is smaller than a human thumb.

AWESOME!

POLE-LAND

Daniel Baraniuk of Gdansk, Poland, won over $20,000 by sitting on top of a pole for

196 DAYS

and nights! His little "Pole"-land was a platform measuring only 16 inches by 24 inches, on top of a pole

8 FEET HIGH.

He was allowed to come down for 10 minutes every two hours, but for the most part he was up there from May to November 2002.

Magician Rick Smith Jr. of Cleveland, Ohio, can throw a single playing card 216 feet. You try it: It's a neat trick!

In 2008, the town square of Ravensburg, Germany, was covered by a jigsaw puzzle measuring 6,500 square feet! The puzzle took 15,000 people just five hours to piece together.

The ground shook in Indianapolis, Indiana, in 2005 when 1,072 people all performed a handstand at the same time!

TURN OVER IF YOU DARE, TO SEE TERRIFYING FEATS ON NIAGARA FALLS

53

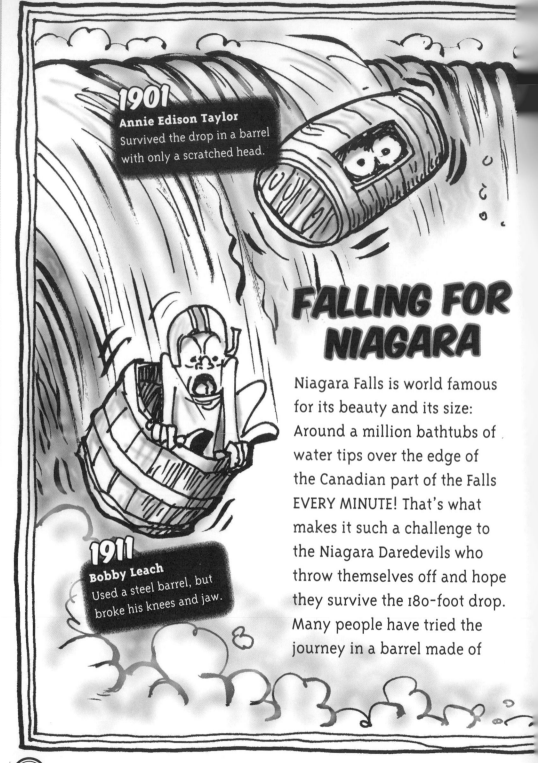

1901
Annie Edison Taylor
Survived the drop in a barrel with only a scratched head.

1911
Bobby Leach
Used a steel barrel, but broke his knees and jaw.

FALLING FOR NIAGARA

Niagara Falls is world famous for its beauty and its size: Around a million bathtubs of water tips over the edge of the Canadian part of the Falls EVERY MINUTE! That's what makes it such a challenge to the Niagara Daredevils who throw themselves off and hope they survive the 180-foot drop. Many people have tried the journey in a barrel made of

1961
Nathan Boya
Dropped over in a steel ball wrapped in rubber. Wasn't injured but was fined $100.

wood, some with a metal or plastic one, others in a giant ball or just on their own. Lots don't survive, but the ones who do get a taste of fame (and a big fine, as it's illegal to try it).

2003
Kirk Jones
No barrel at all! Swam safely to shore but was fined $2,300 and banned from Canada forever!

Loony toons

It's not enough for world-class violinist Drew Tretick to play beautifully—he likes to play precariously, too. Although he plays with world-famous orchestras, and has performed everywhere from Downtown Disney to Las Vegas, he is most noticeable when he's bowing out tunes on top of his unicycle!

Three minutes is long enough to watch the ads on TV, or for Hazel Tindall of Shetland, Scotland, to knit 255 stitches.

MIND YOUR STEP!

Pilot Mike Howard took a walk 4,000 feet up in the sky, from one hot-air balloon to another. The balloons were tied together and connected by a thin beam for Mike to walk along. He couldn't even enjoy the view, though, as he decided to make his challenge harder and do the air-walk wearing a blindfold!

MUSCLE MAN

One of the world's strongest men is Bill Kazmaier of Burlington, Wisconsin. He was the first man to win the

WORLD'S STRONGEST MAN

title three times in a row, and he can pull a bus even when it's full of schoolchildren. He can also lift a boy off the ground, using a rope, with his little finger!

flipping good

Robert Souris of Hollywood, California, is fantastic at front flips: He can jump a distance of 16 feet and clear a line of 16 children lying on the ground. The gymnast lines up his targets, takes a long run up, and forward flips in mid-air right over the top of the children without touching any of them.

Firas al Mualla swam 68 miles across the Mediterranean Sea, from Cyprus to his homeland Syria. He took just 42 hours and didn't stop swimming once.

WATCH ME!

Praveen Kumar Sehrawat is a teen celebrity in his home country of India. He can perform all sorts of party tricks, including

EATING 170 CHILIES

in just over five minutes. He can hammer a nail into his nose without hurting himself, and is able to suck up milk through his nose and then squirt it up to 12 feet out of his eye!

The high life

How long could you spend cooped up in a moving cable car? In 2004, in Singapore, 33 couples attempted to live in the tiny space, nearly 300 feet in the air, for a whole week. They were allowed out for only ten minutes each day to go to the bathroom. Nineteen of the teams lasted the whole seven days, but suffered from motion sickness, claustrophobia, and the intense heat and humidity.

Kenyan strongman Patrick Chege has a tough party trick. He lets heavy trucks drive right over his chest, then stands up to show he's totally unhurt!

Going with the flow

Riding the big one is a supreme thrill for a surfer, but C.J. Kanuha has taken it one wave farther... in April 2008, he surfed within 20 feet of Hawaii's

KILAUEA VOLCANO

lava spill. The molten rock pours into the ocean and heats it to as much as 400°F. Kanuha scalded his feet and the wax on his surfboard melted!

Springing into action

Ioan-Veniamin Oprea is a human slinky! He wears a giant, brightly colored tube and moves and dances like a slinky toy. The Romanian's circus acrobatic training helps him perform all sorts of tumbles, turns, flips and rolls, and audiences around the world are fascinated by his routines.

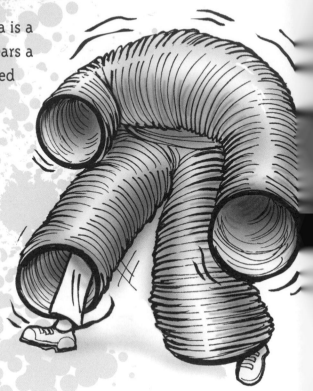

Krishna Gopal Shrivestava is a human tow boat! In 1999, he pulled a boat weighing 270 tons for 49 feet through Calcutta Harbor, using only his teeth!

IN A SPIN

Aichi Ono showed off his super spins at a shopping mall in Hong Kong in December 2007. The 18-year-old from Japan can spin on his head, using his body to gain speed and spin faster. Aichi can spin more than 100 times in a minute.

Wheelie long time

Keiichi Iwasaki left his home in Japan in 2001 to cycle around the country—and never went back! He and his trusty Raleigh Shopper bike have since covered at least

28,000 MILES

and visited 37 countries, taking the super-cyclist all the way across Asia and Europe. Along the way, he climbed Mount Everest, and was arrested in India, robbed by pirates, and attacked by a dog with rabies (a nasty illness) in Tibet.

Magic spells

As if it's not enough knowing big words, nine-year-old Aaron Zweig of Randolph, New Jersey, can spell them, too. He shocked his teacher with a word from the Middle Ages that means a person who can predict the future, and then spelled it out loud in his fourth-grade class. The word?

Ornicopytheobibliopsychocrystarroscioaero-genethliometeoroaustrohieroanthropoichthy-opyrosiderochpnomyoalectryoophiobotanope-gobydrorhabdocrithoaleuroalphitohalomolyb-doclerobeloaxinocoscinodactyliogeolithopes-sopsephocatoptrotephraoneirochiroonychodac-tyloarithstichooxogeloscogastrogyrocerobleto-nooenosapulinaniac.

It contains 309 letters and he spelled it perfectly!

Mike Hagan of Whitehall, Montana, pulled a wheelie on his tractor for 35 minutes in July 2008.

George Adrian from Indianapolis, Indiana, picked 30,000 apples in one day's work. That's 3,750 apples an hour, or more than an apple a second without stopping.

SPLASH NEWS

29 FEET IN THE AIR

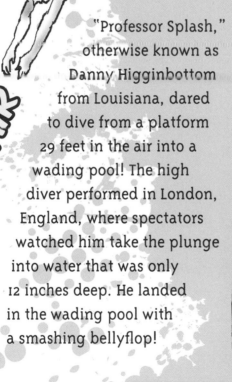

"Professor Splash," otherwise known as Danny Higginbottom from Louisiana, dared to dive from a platform 29 feet in the air into a wading pool! The high diver performed in London, England, where spectators watched him take the plunge into water that was only 12 inches deep. He landed in the wading pool with a smashing bellyflop!

WAY TO LIVE...

On the box

Does your mom say you watch too much TV? Tell her about Chris Dean and Mike Dudek from Grand Rapids, Michigan. The teenagers watched non-stop for 52 hours in August 2004!

AMAZING!

Do the twist

In July 2005, nearly 1,500 students from Temasek Secondary School in Singapore turned their hand to balloon modeling. Their aim was to make as many different balloon shapes as possible, and they managed 16,380 models including flowers, giraffes, and dogs.

Suffering ups and downs

Bungee jumper Mike Heard from New Zealand jumped 131 feet off Auckland Harbor Bridge in August 2008— 103 times! He was bungee-ing for 24 hours, starting off diving head first toward the water, but later jumping feet first as his top half was getting too wet!

WILD

Hard deal

How good is your memory? Test yourself against Ben Pridmore from Derby, England, who can remember the order of a whole deck of shuffled playing cards in just 30 seconds!

Grape expectations

It's easy to throw a grape and catch it in your mouth, right? Well, not necessarily, but lots of people can do it with practice. Beat this though: In East Boston, Massachusetts, in 1991, Paul J. Travilla caught a grape that had been thrown to him from 327½ feet away! No wonder he's known as "The Grape Catcher."

Man or mermaid?

How long can you hold your breath underwater for? Don't try to beat Peter Colat. In 2010, the freediver held his breath underwater for 19 minutes and 21 seconds in St. Gallen, Switzerland.

In 2006, Franz Muellner from Austria held a helicopter weighing 4,000 pounds on his shoulders for an incredible 33.6 seconds.

Window wiper

Terry Burrows is a wow of a window cleaner. In Birmingham, England, in 2005, he cleaned and wiped three windows in under ten seconds.

Passing the puck

We'd bet that Mike Nabuurs had arm ache after his air hockey marathon—in June 2005, the Canadian played for 48 hours without stopping.

Rock-a-bye

Here's a snoozy challenge... in August 2005, Suresh Joachim from Mississauga, Ontario, rocked non-stop in a rocking chair for 3 days, 3 hours, 3 minutes and 3 seconds—without falling asleep. He ate small amounts, and drank water and energy drinks, but made sure he didn't need to stop rocking to use the bathroom.

QUICKER THAN QUICK

Anthony Kelly has black belts in seven martial arts, and has practiced so hard that his reactions are fast enough to catch arrows as they fly past him. The Australian can also catch paintballs—28 of them if he's watching, or 11 if he's blindfolded. And he can punch ten times a second: Faster than his hero Bruce Lee.

In 1981, Canadian Jay Cochrane spent 21 days balancing on a high wire in San Juan, Puerto Rico.

HEAD BANGER

Dan Wilson from Lodi, California, has a smashing time with his party trick—literally. He uses his forehead to break plates, bottles, boards, and bricks. To prepare, he psyches himself up for two hours, concentrating his energy on a single spot on his forehead, only the size of a quarter. His record is a cracking 64 dinner plates in 41 seconds, achieved in 2007.

BIG JUMPERS

If you think jumping out of a plane is crazy, take a look at this lot. One hundred skydivers hurled themselves from five planes and hooked up to make a huge diamond in the sky. It took

SEVEN YEARS

to plan and practice, and is much more dangerous than solo parachuting, as it's easy to get tangled. The jumpers covered the size of a football field for

12 SECONDS

in the air and had only 11 minutes between jumping and landing to get everyone in the correct position.

ON A ROLL

Chester Fried from South River, New Jersey, started roller skating when he was seven. Now the sixty-something skater owns over 300 pairs of roller skates, and has visited every roller-skating rink in the U.S.A.—that's more than 300 rinks in all.

India's Paramjit Singh is a happy clappy: He can clap his hands over 11,600 times in an hour!

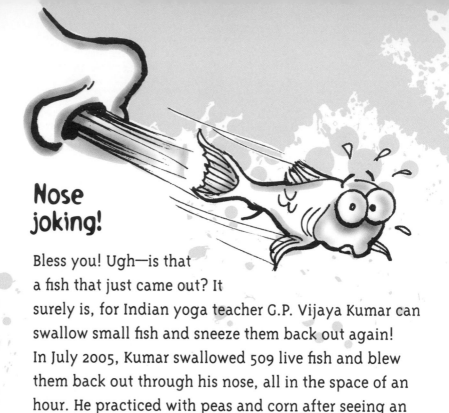

Nose joking!

Bless you! Ugh—is that a fish that just came out? It surely is, for Indian yoga teacher G.P. Vijaya Kumar can swallow small fish and sneeze them back out again! In July 2005, Kumar swallowed 509 live fish and blew them back out through his nose, all in the space of an hour. He practiced with peas and corn after seeing an American, Kevin Cole, do the trick with spaghetti.

Sword throat

The art of sword swallowing can take years to perfect. Roderick Russell, from Burlington, Vermont, practiced three times a day for a year before daring to do his act in front of an audience. Now he can swallow blades that are

24 INCHES LONG

even though the average adult esophagus (the tube from your mouth to your stomach) is only 12 to 15 inches long.

CRAZY CARTWHEELS

Don Claps from Broomfield, Colorado, must be dizzy by the time he's finished performing. He can do over 1,200 cartwheels in a row! He's even learned how to drink while he cartwheels, by holding the cup between his teeth, letting the water into his mouth as his hands head for the floor, and then swallowing on the next rotation.

Mite-y man

Centipede-lover Boontawee Siengwong of Bangkok, Thailand, decided to set up house with 1,000 of the

VENOMOUS CRITTERS

in a room measuring just 10 feet by 13 feet. The glass container had all the creature comforts of a bed, toilet, TV, fan, and refrigerator, but also contained 1,000 centipedes to stop him getting too comfortable. He spent 28 days and nights inside, and the centipedes were free to walk all over him with their hundreds of tiny feet.

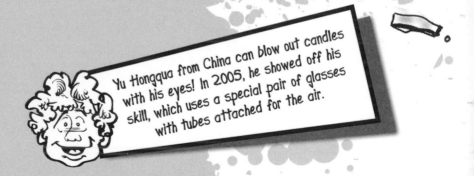

Yu Hongqua from China can blow out candles with his eyes! In 2005, he showed off his skill, which uses a special pair of glasses with tubes attached for the air.

High tea

If you had looked high in the sky in Brussels in April 2006 you might have seen an unusual sight. Twenty-two Belgian chefs were strapped into racing-car seats and winched 165 feet into the air to enjoy a three-course alfresco meal!

SUCH A BLAST!

This performance will blow you away! U.S. entertainer Allison Bly, or "The Dynamite Lady," climbs into her "Coffin of Death" where crowds watch her blown up. Allison wears only a helmet and stars-and-stripes shorts and top, but survives an explosion equal to the detonation of two sticks of dynamite. She has done it over 1,500 times, but her worst injuries have been burns, concussion, and the occasional broken bone.

HIGH-CLIMBING SPIDERMAN

Eiffel Tower

What's the highest you've climbed? Maybe you've been up the Empire State Building? So has Alain Robert—but he went up the outside! He has climbed up over 60 tall buildings, using only special climbing shoes to help him grip to glass, concrete, and metal.

He's also climbed the 1,482-foot Petronas Towers in Kuala Lumpur, Malaysia, and France's Eiffel Tower. It's no surprise he sometimes dresses as Spiderman, the way he crawls up the walls.

Empire State Building

SLOWLY DOES IT

Penny-farthing bicycles aren't built for speed, but they can go the distance, as shown by Joff Summerfield. Joff, from Great Britain, built his own replica penny farthing and rode it around the world, covering

21,976 MILES

in 2½ years. On his journey he passed through 23 countries, was hit by two trucks, camped with crocodiles, and was mugged—but he eventually made it home safely.

YO!

Australian Ben McPhee appeared at the 2010 London Toy Fair to show off his yo-yo talents. Ben, from Newcastle, New South Wales, spun 16 yo-yos at the same time, using his fingers, hooks, his ears, and his teeth to keep all the yo-yos in action at once.

Family day out

Father-and-son performers Johann and Johann Traber from Germany are spectacular tightrope artists. One of their awe-inspiring acts saw them cross 1,900 feet on a tightrope, 525 feet in the air. Not only that, they used a motorbike that dangled from a trapeze! Johann Senior sat on the trapeze and his son rode the motorbike, and they spun over and over 14 times to make their audience really gasp.

India's Amanullah can write different sentences with both hands, at the same time. Even more amazingly, he can write one in English and the other in Tamil!

?TAHW YAS

Can you spell backward? Yeah, yeah:

B–A–C–K–W–A–R–D

Very clever. Raghav Srivathsav from Hyderabad, India, can do it properly. The eight-year-old has been spelling words in reverse since he was three, and can now spell 50 words backward in less than three minutes. He can also do it with phrases: Tell him a line and he'll repeat it back to you, backward, in seconds.

In 1997, in Sri Lanka, Suresh Joachim balanced on one foot for 76 hours: that's 3 days and 4 hours!

WORKS LIKE A CHARM

Sophie Smith from Cheshire, England, is a real charmer—a worm charmer. At only ten years old, she won the World Worm Charming Championships. In half an hour, she

COLLECTED 567 WORMS

by charming them out of the ground. Most competitors coax the worms to the surface by poking a stick or fork into the ground and then hitting it to make vibrations, but some others dance like Elvis, tap dance to the theme from *Star Wars*, or play music to the worms.

Blade safe

The Great Throwdini is one of the world's greatest knife-throwers. He can hurl 144 knives around a human target in only a minute, and has thrown 22 knives in a ladder formation round his live target in under 10 seconds. Throwdini, whose real name is David Adamovich, is a cool catcher, too: He is the first person to complete the Triple Crown, catching a knife, an arrow, and then a speeding bullet in his bare hand.

SSSOUNDS SSSORE

A snake handler in Nanjing, China, can put a snake in his mouth and pull it out of his nose! Once the snake is inside his mouth, he closes his throat so the snake doesn't get swallowed. Instead of heading down, the snake has to head upward, into the air cavity behind his nose, and back down through his nostril. Gruesome but fascinating!

THE BUS WORD

Evil Knievel used to jump over buses on his motorbike—now Steve Hudis has leaped over a row of bikes in a bus! The stunt driver zoomed through a fireball in a school bus weighing

28,000 POUNDS!

It reached a height of 109 feet, cleared 15 motorcycles, and crashed to the ground allowing Steve to walk away safely.

NO LIMITS...

Chance encounter

Brent Carey wrestled an alligator to save the life of his girlfriend's dog, named Chance. The alligator appeared from a lake in a park in Charleston, South Carolina, and grabbed Chance between its teeth. It was heading back to the water to gobble down its tasty snack when Brent jumped on the back of the 10-foot-long monster, and managed to get Chance out of its jaws.

Pilot Robert Magniccari from Rockaway, New Jersey, took off in his plane and landed at a nearby airport 190 times in 24 hours!

Face lift

Luo Deyuan from Guiyang, China, is a martial-arts expert with some unusual tricks. He can lift two buckets of water using his eyelids, and also uses his lids to tow a car weighing a ton. He pulled another vehicle along a road by fastening a rope to a piercing in his neck, and he can stop an electric fan spinning using his tongue.

PAINFUL!

Ground control

Workers at a mill in Pembrokeshire, Wales, wove a picnic blanket that was big enough to cover four tennis courts. It weighed a ton and took three weeks to make.

Banded about

Joel Waul of Lauderhill, Florida, has made a ball made of rubber bands that weighs half a ton and is taller than most men! It contains 780,000 rubber bands and smells so strongly that Joel had to keep it outside his house. That's no longer a problem as it's now in Ripley's Warehouse in Florida, Orlando.

Wacky races

Students from Temasek Polytechnic, Singapore, are "wheely" keen on human wheelbarrows. In April 2009, 74 of them linked together in one long wheelbarrow chain, and 1,378 of them paired up for a giant wheelbarrow race.

Super-shooter Randy Oitker from Plainville, Illinois, shot five arrows in a row and hit five targets that were only as big as a coin.

ONE-MAN CIRCUS

The Amazing Blazing Tyler Fyre is a one-man circus show! He can breathe fire, glass, razor blades and live insects, swallow swords, hammer nails up his nose, juggle machetes, and has escaped from chains while hanging upside down 6 feet above the stage in a straitjacket. He trained as a circus performer, learning juggling, high wire, trapeze, and fire-eating, after realizing during childhood that he could squirt liquids and even spaghetti and meatballs out of his nose.

What to wear?

It's not a question that bothered Austin D. Crow
one day in 2007—he just wore everything! The
12-year-old from Easthampton, Massachusetts, took

THREE HOURS TO GET DRESSED

and by the end was wearing 168 T-shirts! His
starting weight was just III pounds, but fully dressed
he topped the scales at 190 pounds and was too wide
to fit through the doorway.

BACKWARD BABBLE

Say what? Samir
Tandon from India
can talk and read
backward: He can
even sing songs
backward from
finish to start.

Double science

... and then some! Giovanni Cogollo took a science
lesson in Turbaco, northern Colombia, that lasted for
74 hours in 2008. He taught 120 students from Friday
to Monday in order to raise money for charity.

BALANCE OF POWER

Eskil Ronningsbakken certainly has a head for heights! He has been training for

30 YEARS

and it seems no act is too scary for him to try. Eskil's most difficult stunt was riding a bike upside down on a tightrope,

3,000 FEET

in the air. He has also balanced on a giant ice cube, perched on a rope above a glacier, and balanced on a steel ring on the edge of a cliff. Eskil has been practicing his skills since he was a child and saw on TV an Indian yogi doing a balancing act.

Teenage fiction

Read any good books lately? Okay then—have you written any good books lately? Flavia Bujor has, and she's only a teenager! She was just 12 when she wrote her first novel, and has since had it published in over 20 countries. Romanian-born Flavia lives in Paris and started work on her second novel soon after seeing her first book in print.

Mighty man

Chad Netherland, from Myrtle Beach, South Carolina, is a martial arts expert with hands of steel—or so it seems. In 2009, he chopped through 16 blocks of ice stacked together, with a single strike. He can also rip packs of cards and licence plates into pieces, and has smashed 50 blocks of ice in just 19 seconds. He has also held two airplanes, preventing them taking off for over a minute, by holding them back with his super-strength arms.

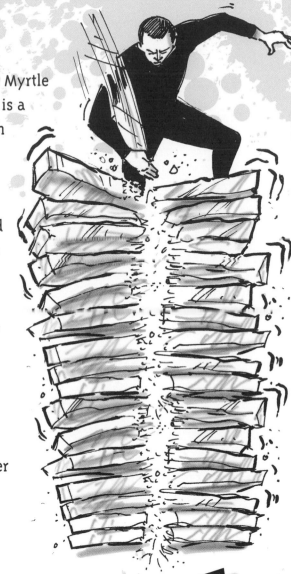

American comedian Mike Heeman spent 24 hours telling non-stop jokes in 1992. He managed to get through 12,682 giggletastic gags.

SHEAR DELIGHT

Doug Rathke of Hutchinson, Minnesota, is a super-shearer. He can shear a single sheep in less than 2½ minutes, and won first place in an international sheep-shearing competition by shearing

607 SHEEP

in 24 hours. He must have been completely shorn out!

LOOK, NO HANDS!

Matt Hoffman is a brilliant BMX bandit. Matt from Oklahoma City was the first person to do a no-handed 900. That involves taking off at the top of a ramp, spinning the bike 2½ times while holding on with just his legs and feet, and then landing on both tires without falling off. Pretty cool, huh?

The self-named "Lord of Pumpkins," Stephen Clarke of Haverton, Pennsylvania, can carve a face into a pumpkin in under 25 seconds.

91

Treading on eggshells

Not jumping over eggs, but jumping ON them—without breaking them—Joseph Darby from Dudley, England, could do "eggs"-actly that! He was holder of the world jumping championship from 1882 to 1892, and could jump on and off an open basket of eggs so fast he didn't break any of them.

Alesya Goulevich knows how to hula: In April 2004 she spun 100 hula hoops at the same time at the Big Apple Circus in Boston.

COME OVER EAR!

Zhang Xinquan's right ear is bigger than his left, but there's a good reason for that—he uses it for pulling trains! He has been practicing for years, so one ear has stretched, but in 2005 the practice paid off and he pulled a train weighing 24 tons along a track for 130 feet. He also uses his ears to pull cars, while walking on eggs—without breaking them!

Come fly with me

... er, no thanks—seeing as you built your own airplane! That's right: Peng Cong from Chongqing, China, built his own aircraft at a

COST OF $27,000.

He learned how from books and the Internet, and it did really fly on just his second launch, reaching 1,000 feet up in the sky.

Prrrrrrp! In July 2005, in Bowie, Maryland, nearly 4,500 baseball fans sat on whoopee cushions at the same time. Parptastic!

STAIR-CRAZY

Bernadette Hallfeld Duychak never takes the elevator if she can avoid it—because she just loves climbing stairs! In August 2005, she climbed the stairs of her 54-story condominium in Chicago, Illinois, more than 55 times in 24 hours. That's around 40,000 stairs in a day! To start with, she could hardly manage 20 floors, but now says she climbs over 2,000 floors every week.

RIPLEY's
TRAVELING IN STYLE

These two are well-traveled: Not that you'd know it from their smart suits. Heath Buck and Doug Campbell met in Hong Kong and decided to travel back to London, across Asia, in tuxedos, to raise money for charity.

Dressed and ready to go.

Snowy conditions in Kyrgyzstan.

Lots of local attention.

Becoming tribe members in Vietnam.

Wrestling in India.

Success! Five months later in London, England, still in tuxes!

95

RIPLEY'S
DID YOU KNOW???

This looks tricky: Line dancing on stilts! In January 2006, 34 members of the Lieder Youth Theatre Company in New South Wales, Australia, managed it for over 6 minutes.

You're never too old to learn something new, as proved by Fred Hale Sr. of New York. He was 104 when he got his driver's licence!

Robert G. Davis drove his snowmobile through Maine and Canada for 60 days in 2008, clocking up 12,163 miles through the snow.

Welshman Dave Cornthwaite traveled 3,618 miles from Perth to Brisbane—on a skateboard! That's the width of Australia—and it took him 90 days.

Harry Egger from Austria is a world-class extreme skier. The sport involves zooming down super-steep slopes at top speed: Harry reached 155 mph in 1999.

Ripey's
Believe It or Not!®

BRRM!

ZANY TRANSPORT STORIES, FUN, AND FACTS

Illustrated by John Graziano

PUBLISHING

Publishing Director Anne Marshall
Editorial Director Becky Miles
Art Director Sam South
Senior Designer Michelle Foster
Assistant Editor Charlotte Howell
Design Ark Creative
Reprographics Juice Creative

BRRM!

transport

You won't believe the ways people get around when you dip inside this fun-packed book! Check out the car covered in Post-it® notes, the bike shaped like a burger, and the plane that flies upside down, plus many more! **It's Ripley's Shout Outs!**

INTRODUCING...
JOHN GRAZIANO

John, Ripley's very own cartoonist, has drawn every cartoon in this wacky book of crazy transport stories.

A new Ripley's cartoon has been produced every day for the past 90 years by a dedicated Ripley's cartoonist. John is only the eighth person to take on this role. Amazingly, he got himself the job 25 years after sending his drawings to Ripley's as a teenager!

SPEEDY QUESTIONS!

1. Q: What tools do you use for your drawings?
A: My actual drawings are done the old-fashioned way: with pencil, pen and ink, and brush and ink to paper. For airbrushing and coloring, I use a Wacom digital tablet.

2. Q: If you hadn't become an artist what would you be?
A: I actually wanted to be a paleontologist and dig up fossils! I do that as a hobby though.

3. Q: If you could choose a method of travel from this book which one would it be?
A: In the head of the Robosaurus looks fun!

4. Q: Can you ride a bike?
A: Yes!

Ripley's ON THE CASE

Mazda have the solution to waiting in line at the airport. Instead of collecting your luggage and then loading it into a taxi, why not UNLOAD it and drive away on it?! The idea came from a Mazda engineer in 1991, who designed a car that fits entirely inside a suitcase. It unfolds and can be put together in about 20 seconds, and driven away at 27 mph. See ya!

VARROOOOOM!

WATER FEATURE

John Melling from Cornwall, England, has a yacht in his yard. He spent five years building the 26-foot-wide boat himself, always knowing it would be too big to get it out of the garden when it was finished.

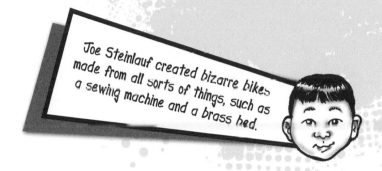

Joe Steinlauf created bizarre bikes made from all sorts of things, such as a sewing machine and a brass bed.

Made of money

Ken and Annie Burkitt of Niagara Falls, Ontario, Canada, certainly knew how to make an eye-catching vehicle. Their creations included a double-decker London bus covered with

gold-plated British pennies, and a limousine decorated with

gold coins. Their "American Icon" Mini Cooper is covered with over a million Swarovski crystals in 50 shades to create U.S. emblems such as Mount Rushmore and the national flag.

STICKY SITUATION

Walt from Washington D.C. loves a practical joke better than most people, but his colleagues had the last laugh when they completely covered his car with Post-it® notes. Scott Ableman and 12 other co-workers took under two hours—and 14,000 brightly colored notes—to stick up Walt's beloved Jaguar. As always, Walt saw the funny side, and even drove the car home to show his family, after he'd cleared the windows to drive safely.

Monorail mad

Kim Pedersen of Fremont, California, is so mad on monorails that he's built one in his backyard. He first sketched his plans when he was at high school, but his parents wouldn't give him permission to build in their yard. Now he's all grown up with a home of his own, he has finally fulfilled his dream… he spent five years and $4,000 dollars constructing 300 feet of track that is up to 8 feet high above his plants and pool.

A teenager in Toronto failed her driving test in 2001 when she returned to the test center, and accidentally pressed the accelerator, and crashed into six cars.

Farm-ula one

Chinese brothers Zhao Xiushun and Zhao Baoguo have built their own Formula 1 racing car out of pieces of metal found around their farm. The brothers, who live in Tangshan, have spent 20 years putting together the race car, using items such as steel doors, cooking pots, and bits of bicycles. Amazingly, their F1 masterpiece can achieve a top speed of 100 mph!

Foot off the gas

Tom Fewins and Lara Lockwood, from Oxfordshire, England, traveled right around the planet in 297 days, without using a single airplane. The pair covered over

44,000 MILES

through 19 countries using buses, trains, cars, boats, bicycles, mopeds, and even an elephant. Their journey generated around two-thirds less carbon dioxide than if they had flown it in a plane.

DEAD FAST

Roger Fox, a retired deputy sheriff from Fairborn, Ohio, has built his own coffin car. It is made from two caskets and parts taken from 1960s "muscle cars." It took four years to build and Roger loves it so much that he wants to be buried in it.

Crazy bones

B.J. Zander from Minnesota has covered her Volvo in animal bones! She calls it her "Mercedes Bonz" and has spent four years collecting beef and chicken bones from friends and butchers. Now her car is shielded by nearly 1,000 bones.

DRIVING THE PLANK

Talented sculptor Livio de Marchi of Venice, Italy, has carved several cars from wood, and because wood floats, he also "drives" them along the Venice canals! His models include a Ferrari F50, a VW Beetle, a Fiat Topolino, and a 1937 Jaguar that is powered by a 20-horsepower engine.

High and mighty

Watching a monster truck in action is great fun, but would you believe they can jump over 26 feet high and 130 feet along? That's like 14 cars side by side.

INCREDIBLE!

Car cash

Paul Brant sure knows how to save: In 1994, he had collected enough quarters to pay $36,000 for a car and a truck, in cash. By 2007, he had once again saved enough coins—quarters and dollars this time—to buy a new Dodge truck costing $25,000.

Flight mite

The Pixelito is a minuscule helicopter, created by Alexander van de Rostyne in Brussels, Belgium. It weighs only ¼ ounce and is controlled by infra-red signals.

WOW!

Traffic pile-up

The Boston University Bridge in Boston, Massachusetts, is one of the few bridge layouts where you can find a boat floating under a train, which is driving under a car, with maybe an airplane flying over all of them!

Bendy bike

Some people can fold
themselves up into tiny spaces... so
can Dominic Hargreaves's bicycle. The student from
London has invented "The Contortionist," a bike that
folds down to the size of one wheel, and can be pulled
along using its handlebars in restricted areas. The
wacky racer can be collapsed in 20 seconds and wheeled
onto trains or along corridors to help commuters.

AWESOME!

The fastest recorded speed on a pedal bike is 167 mph, achieved by Dutch cyclist Fred Rompelberg in 1995 by cycling in the slip stream of a dragster car.

Dairy dragster

The humble milk float is best known for its lack
of speed, but Welsh racing driver Richard Rozhon
managed to coax 73 mph out of the electric engine at a
milk float speed trial in Leicestershire, England, in 2003.

Pigs might fly

In 1783, in Versailles, Paris, France, a rooster, a duck,
and a sheep became the first creatures ever to
fly in a basket hanging from
a hot-air balloon.

AMAZING!

KEEP ON TRUCKIN'

Monster trucks are BIG business! Fans
love to watch the huge beasts pounding
around a track and over piles of trashed cars,
making metal mincemeat of anything in their
path. World-famous Bigfoot trucks make a
deafening din and ride on tires that are
10 feet tall and weigh 2,400 pounds EACH!
Bigfoot 5   stands 15 feet 6 inches

tall and is nearly as wide. It was created by Bob Chandler of St. Louis, Missouri, who bought the enormous tires, big enough to fit a grown man inside, from a junkyard.

Airplay

John David can see the Swiss Alps or the New York skyline, without ever leaving his own home. He spent eight years converting his spare bedroom into an exact copy of the cockpit of a Boeing 747, complete with 6-foot "windows" showing views from around the world. It also has perfect sound effects and includes every single switch included on a real Boeing 747 plane!

No comfort breaks

British couple Dr. James Shippen and Barbara May drove for

2,000 MILES

without stopping for food, gas, or even the toilet! The pair, from Bromsgrove, England, traveled from northern Scotland to southern Italy in April 2005 using their Indipod invention: an in-car toilet. They took a huge supply of food and depended on helpful gas station workers for refueling.

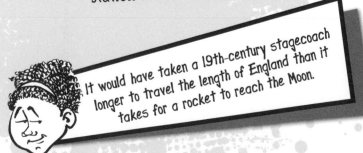

It would have taken a 19th-century stagecoach longer to travel the length of England than it takes for a rocket to reach the Moon.

Ripley's

PARK AND SEEK

What would you do if you had just one parking space but two cars?

You could always install AutoPod... the parking space that's hidden underground!

Simply drive your car into the pod, stand to one side, press a button...

and watch your car be lowered into the ground.

The cool car solution was invented by a British company and can be hidden under your driveway or in your yard. Neat!

ALL ABOARD!

Ever hitched a ride on your dad's handlebars? There's no need, if your dad is Roger Dumas. He spent

OVER 20 YEARS

putting together a bicycle that would fit all of his family at once. It's a double-decker contraption made from bits of 150 other bikes, and is 140 feet long. In 2000, he gathered together all 55 members of his family, and they rode together for more than half a mile.

George Selden patented the automobile in 1895, but never actually produced a working car.

Be prepared!

Paul Stender is never too far from the toilet when
nature calls. The U.S. mechanic's Port-O-Jet is a
washroom on wheels, complete with the original toilet
seat inside for the driver to sit on. The wooden hut has
a 750-pound jet engine taken from a Boeing airplane,
which powers the portapotty at up to 70 mph.
It also throws out fireballs from the back,
up to 30 feet behind!

DREAM MACHINES...

Wheely keen

K. Sudhakar from Hyderabad, India, is mad about bikes and cars, and has designed and built hundreds of them. He started at the age of 14, and has come up with some crazy creations, from a motorbike that is only 13 inches high, to cars shaped like a helmet, a cricket ball, and a cup and saucer.

CRAZY!

Doing the rounds

A donut, in car-speak, is a 360-degree spin keeping one set of wheels in the same place, usually producing lots of smoke and a circular skid pattern. R.J. Brunow from Australia did 64 donuts in a row in May 2005, at the Queensland Raceway—but destroyed a brand new set of tires by the time he had finished.

The fastest thing in the world is, probably, the world! Our planet travels through space at around 64,000 mph.

Chunky chopper

The Russian Mil Mi-26 helicopter is the heaviest helicopter in the world. The airborne giant can carry 70 to 100 passengers or 24 tons of cargo.

AWESOME!

For the last 40 years more bicycles have been produced each year than cars. It's thought that around 100 million bikes are made every year.

Rare beetle

The "Flutterbug" isn't a beetle that can be found in any book on insects: It's the creation of artist Konnie May from Ashland, Oregon. She has painted the body of her VW Beetle with brightly colored butterflies, and attached antennae and wings that even flap at the push of a button.

Pygmy plane

The world's smallest jet is the Bede BD-5J Microjet, with a wingspan of just 17 feet. It is owned by Juan Jimenez of San Juan, Puerto Rico, and can fly at a speed of 300 mph.

Flying economy?

Charles McKinley decided to save money on his airfare, so he traveled from Newark, New Jersey, to Dallas, Texas, packed in a crate in the plane's cargo hold. When it was discovered what he had done, he was fined so much that he could have bought himself a first- class ticket for the same flight!

INCREDIBLE!

Going green

The WorldFirst Formula 3 car is the ultimate eco-friendly racing car. Its steering wheel is made from a carrot-based material, it has a seat made from flax fiber and soybean oil foam, and potato starch in its rearview mirrors. It was developed at Warwick University, England, and can reach 125 mph even when cornering. All that, and it is fueled by a biodiesel made from local chocolate waste products.

SHARK ON WHEELS

Tom Kennedy made a car that looks like a shark—including fins, razor-sharp teeth, gills, and a moving tail. The shark is known as

"RIPPER"

and its body is made from foam insulation and steel. Underneath is a 1982 Nissan, and inside Tom, an artist from San Francisco, has added blue fluorescent lights and hung glowing rubber fish to help passengers feel what it might be like if you were actually eaten by a shark!

FAST FOOD

Fast food doesn't get much faster than Harry Sperl's burger bike! Harry can often be seen racing around Daytona Beach, Florida, on his tasty trike. Underneath the fiberglass and Styrofoam burger body is an 1100cc Harley Davidson, and it even has onion and tomato rings on the wheels, a melted cheese fender, and ketchup bottles as shock covers!

Kid caper

Don't try this at home! Five-year-old Tanishk Boyas from India had been learning to drive by copying his father at the wheel. He always practiced with an adult, until one day his younger cousin was hurt in a fall, so Tanishk drove him to the hospital without any grown-up help.

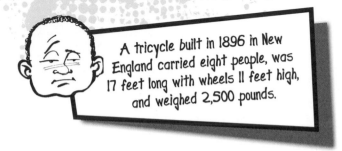

A tricycle built in 1896 in New England carried eight people, was 17 feet long with wheels 11 feet high, and weighed 2,500 pounds.

Root of the problem

Several huge oak trees were transported 500 yards to make way for a new chain store being built on their land. New laws protecting old trees meant that the store, in Auburndale, Florida, had to pay over

$100,000

to dig out and move the trees. The largest was 120 years old and weighed a massive 353 tons.

MEALS ON WHEELS

Feeling hungry but in a real rush? Perry Watkins from Northamptonshire, England, has created a roadworthy table, with six place settings, candlesticks, an ice bucket, and even a dummy racing driver seated and ready to dine. The actual driver sits underneath the table, with his head poking out beneath a roast chicken. The table is built around a sports car chassis with a Land Rover engine, and has reached test speeds of

103 MPH!

No wonder it's nicknamed Fast Food!

ROCKIN' ROADSTER

Yes, you can believe your eyes. This is a motorbike in the shape of a guitar! It was built by Ray Nelson of San Jose, California, in 1981, and in the following year he rode it solo from

SAN FRANCISCO TO NEW YORK.

It's probably the only guitar to be ridden coast to coast, and is sure to have got a few second glances as it zoomed past!

Toy racer

Dirk Auer reached 65 mph driving a toy car! The German took to the wheel of the jet-powered toy, which had its original steering, but added carbon fiber reinforcement on the bodywork, and the engine from a model airplane. It had no brakes, though, so Dirk had to use his feet to slow down and stop.

E.G. Hadley from Caspur, Wyoming, covered his car with nearly 38,000 stamps from 60 different countries.

Found in transit

Hiroshi Nohara, a tourist from Tokyo, moved in to Mexico City airport instead of returning to his Japanese home. He loved the airport's Terminal 1 so much that he stayed there for nearly

FOUR MONTHS

and became famous for it! He was given food, blankets, and clothing by other tourists and by the fast-food restaurants in the building.

Train of events

Edwin Gallart was the least popular passenger possible in October 2003 when he dropped his cell phone down the

TRAIN TOILET

and then got his arm stuck trying to fish it out. The train—and all those queuing behind it—was held up for hours while rescue workers took apart the whole toilet to get him unstuck.

Bobby Hunt's stage bike is only 8 inches tall, and measures 3 inches from one wheel to the other, but Bobby can actually ride it!

Bike with brains

In 2009, British Olympic cyclist Chris Boardman unveiled

"THE BIKE OF THE FUTURE."

It has features such as puncture-proof, self-inflating tires, an unbreakable locking device, a mini computer in the handlebars to count calories as the pedals are pushed, and solar panels to charge a battery so the bike can be motorized if the rider gets tired.

A WING AND A PRAYER

Felix Baumgartner has flown 22 miles across the English Channel, without an airplane! The Austrian extreme sports fanatic used only a carbon fiber wing measuring almost 6 feet to glide across the water after jumping from a plane at 30,000 feet. He needed oxygen to breathe so high up, and reached speeds of 225 mph on the way down. He was happy to reach France and be able to parachute safely to the ground.

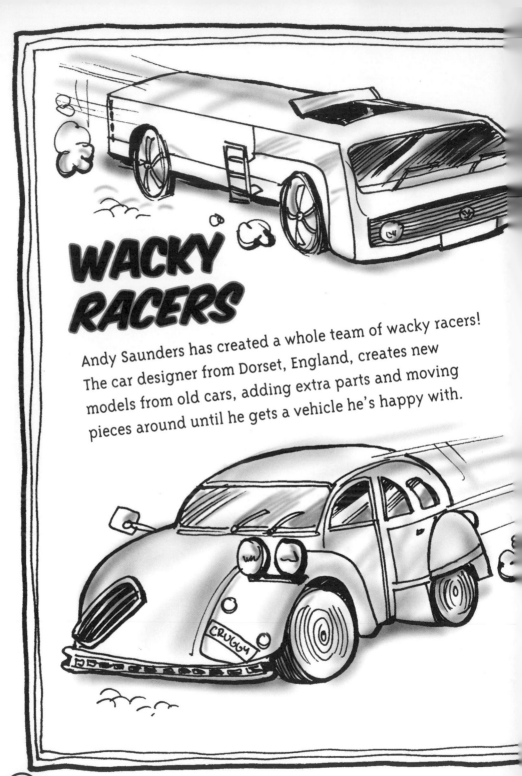

WACKY RACERS

Andy Saunders has created a whole team of wacky racers! The car designer from Dorset, England, creates new models from old cars, adding extra parts and moving pieces around until he gets a vehicle he's happy with.

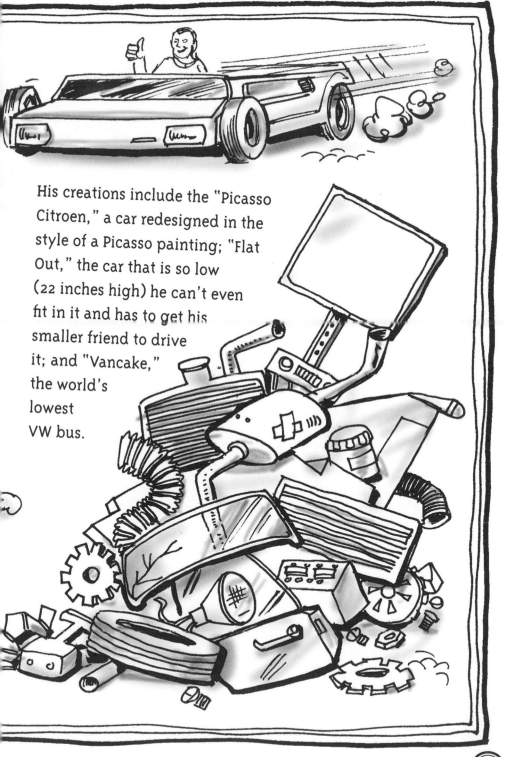

His creations include the "Picasso Citroen," a car redesigned in the style of a Picasso painting; "Flat Out," the car that is so low (22 inches high) he can't even fit in it and has to get his smaller friend to drive it; and "Vancake," the world's lowest VW bus.

WONDER WHEEL

Is it a car? Is it a motorbike? Is it a bit of both? It's the Mclean Monowheel and it's a sight to see! Its inventor, Kerry McLean of Walled Lake, Michigan, worked as a welder until his single-wheeled vehicle hit the big time, and now he tours the world showing it off. The Monowheel is hard to control, with a V8 engine and speeds of up to 50 mph, but Kerry has had plenty of practice.

Bear night!

Japanese scientists have developed a robot teddy bear that sits on a car's dashboard to help the driver. The teddy is

12 INCHES TALL

with moving parts so that it can point in the direction needed. It also talks to help lost drivers find their way, and says, "Watch out!" if the car speeds up or slows down suddenly.

BEST LEGS FORWARD

The Mondo Spider is the creation of designers in Vancouver, British Columbia, Canada, and is an

EIGHT-LEGGED WALKING MACHINE

with a seat for a single rider. It stands 5 feet tall and is powered by a Honda engine. The eight steel legs are moved by hydraulic pumps, and the spider can carry a person along at just under 3 mph.

MILES FROM ANYWHERE

Irvin Gordon from East Patchogue, New York, has clocked up over two million miles in the same car. He bought his Volvo in 1966 and used it for his daily commute of 250 miles until he retired. Now the former science teacher often drives out of state to have lunch, as he loves his car so much.

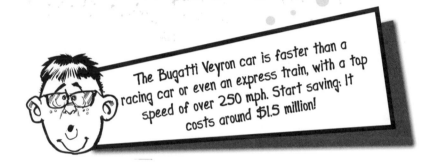

The Bugatti Veyron car is faster than a racing car or even an express train, with a top speed of over 250 mph. Start saving: It costs around $1.5 million!

Toolbox to takeoff

Peng Cong from Chongqing, China, has spent

$27,000

building his own airplane. He learned everything he needed from books and the Internet, and constructed a plane that's 18 feet long with wings measuring 32 feet across. He successfully flew the plane to an altitude of 1,000 feet on its second attempt.

COOKING ON GAS

That's literally what Josh Harper did on Christmas Day 2002. He overslept and still needed to cook his turkey before arriving at his girlfriend's house, so he fired up his car and cooked the Christmas bird

ON THE ENGINE

as he drove! The journey to Bristol, England, was 90 miles—far enough to cook the bird, but he needed a few more miles to soften the potatoes he planned to eat with it.

Everything to lose

The London transport system records huge
amounts of lost property each year, including over

32,000 BOOKS,

27,000 PURSES, AND

25,000 PIECES OF CLOTHING

that have been left behind. It's
harder to imagine how anyone lost
these items, though: a coffin, a

PROSTHETIC ARM,

a pair of breast implants, a case full
of human teeth, a wheelchair, a
steamed puffer fish, and a life-size
toy gorilla!

The airbags used for
safety in a car inflate
at 200 mph. That's faster
than an airplane's
speed at takeoff.

RIDING HIGH

Michael Mooney of Asheville, North Carolina, sure has a head for heights. He's a high rider who can often be seen cycling his "tall bikes" that measure 6 feet and 12 feet in height. In September 2007, he topped that, big style, by cycling a bike that was higher than a house! The machine was 44 feet tall—bigger than a two-story house plus roof—and Michael pedaled for a few yards before gravity took effect and the bike toppled over.

WAY TO GO...

Secondhand submarine

Tao Xiangli, a laborer from China, has spent a year's wages building his own submarine. It is made from all sorts of things, including metal barrels, with secondhand tools he bought from a market. The sub should dive to 30 feet, and has a periscope, electric motors, and depth-control tanks, and is big enough for just one person.

Ship shape

The *Oasis of the Seas* is one seriously large cruise ship. It has 18 decks, a 750-seat aqua theater, and a six-story climbing wall. Overall it is longer than four soccer pitches.

Switch it off!

The amount of electricity used in just one day in the U.S. would power a car around the world more than 36,000 times.

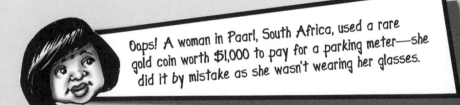

Oops! A woman in Paarl, South Africa, used a rare gold coin worth $51,000 to pay for a parking meter—she did it by mistake as she wasn't wearing her glasses.

Making it big

The record for the largest engine capacity in a production car is held jointly by two cars that are nearly 100 years old. The Peerless 6-60 and the Fageol, both built before 1919, had 13.5-liter engines—bigger than a Volvo FM truck.

Wheel deal

In 1817, Karl von Drais from Germany built and rode the first ever two-wheel bike, called the "draisine." It had no pedals, so the rider simply pushed it along with his feet.

To get to her work as a school teacher in Pueblo, Colorado, Clara Weston waded across the Arkansas River twice a day for four months.

Speed limited

Early mechanical vehicles traveled at walking speed! In England, they were limited to 4 mph until 1896, as they had to follow a man walking ahead, carrying a red flag. The flag was a warning to other road users, and even today "to put up a red flag" means to be careful and proceed with caution.

Bye, bye bikers

Keen motorbike riders can meet their maker in a coffin pulled along by a Harley Davidson motorcycle, thanks to Brit biker Gordon Fitch.

AMAZING!

The first flight was by the Wright brothers and covered 120 feet. That's a shorter distance than the wingspan on a Boeing 747!

Don't freak out...

Taxi driver Harpreet Devi isn't going to crash into oncoming traffic, he's moving in the same direction—but facing backward. Harpeet drives everywhere like this since his car got stuck in reverse gear some years ago. He made the 35 mile-journey home safely, and since then he's covered over 7,500 miles in the same manner. His passengers don't seem to mind!

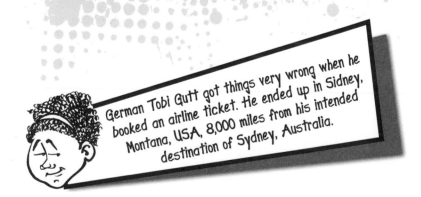

German Tobi Gutt got things very wrong when he booked an airline ticket. He ended up in Sidney, Montana, USA, 8,000 miles from his intended destination of Sydney, Australia.

RIDING ROUND

Going for a cycle ride with friends has taken on a whole new meaning for Eric Staller from Amsterdam, Netherlands. His invention, the CoBi (Conference Bike) fits

SEVEN PEOPLE

at once, seated in a circle. It reaches 15 mph with all seven cyclists pedaling together—but they have to decide which one is in charge of the steering wheel!

Pink mini

Janette Hanson of Macclesfield, England, was so keen for her Mini Cooper to match her favorite pink purse that she paid

$20,000

for custom paintwork.
The purse itself only cost $40!

Reg Pollard from England built a model Rolls-Royce in 1987 made completely from matchsticks—1,016,711 of them!

Model man

Michael Zarnock of Deerfield, New York, can't afford to collect full-size cars, but he does own over

25,000

model cars. Many of them are kept at the Children's Museum in Utica, New York, including more than 8,000 Hot Wheels cars that are his pride and joy!

Ripley's — LET ME OUT!

Ken Imhoff had long dreamed of the day he would drive off in his custom-built Lamborghini. He spent 17 years building the sports car himself in the cellar of his Wisconsin home.

Imagine his horror when he finished the project, and realized he couldn't get it out from its underground workshop!

However, two hours, one digger, and a few missing foundations later...

... he managed to pull out his pride and joy and finally see how it handled!

47

Dennis L. Wheat from Malvern, Arkansas, thought he was lucky to win a car in a raffle—until he found out it was the one he had traded in six years earlier!

Flat tires...

... flat windshield, nearly flat passengers! Rico Beltrame and his sister Angela, from Switzerland, were on safari at the Hluhluwe Umfolozi nature reserve in South Africa when a

6-TON ELEPHANT

wandered over for a closer look at their car. Instead of stopping at a safe distance, the mighty beast leaned on their jeep for five minutes before losing interest and wandering off. Phew!

There are more than 170,000 miles of railroad track in the U.S.A.

CRAZY CRASH

Guests arriving at their friend's house in Massachusetts were shocked to see a car sticking out of the roof! They were gathering for their Fourth of July celebrations, but first had to deal with the Ford Taurus that had crashed into the building. The car drove off an elevated parking lot and straight through the rafters, but fortunately no one was hurt and the celebratory fireworks carried on as planned.

DRIVING FORCE...

Properly a-tired
The world's biggest tires are used on enormous front-end-loader Caterpillar trucks. Each tire costs $30,000, takes three days to make, and uses enough rubber for over 5,000 regular car tires.

Totally driven
Maybe Los Angeles, California, should steal Detroit's "Motortown" nickname? The city of L.A. is the most car-populated metropolis in the world, with 1.8 registered cars for every licensed driver there. Los Angeles County has 10 million people and 10.5 million registered cars, and nearly one-quarter of the land area is taken up by cars.

WILD!

Air miles
The longest journey by powered paraglider was Bob Holloway's 2,580-mile trip in 2004, following the "Lewis and Clark trail" from Astoria, Oregon, to Washington, Missouri.

An entire roller coaster, weighing over 20 tons, was stolen from the back of a truck in Germany in May 2006.

INCREDIBLE!

Homespun spinner

Wu Zhongyuan of Luoyang, Henan Province, China, has built his own helicopter. The 20-year-old has only a basic school education, but figured out how to make the chopper using a motorcycle engine and wooden rotor blades. It took him nearly three months to construct, and he claims it will fly to a height of 2,625 feet.

AMAZING!

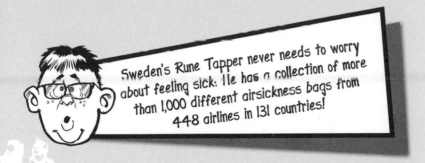

Sweden's Rune Tapper never needs to worry about feeling sick. He has a collection of more than 1,000 different airsickness bags from 448 airlines in 131 countries!

Fare play

Eric Hagen, the owner of Recession Ride Taxi in Essex, Vermont, has an unusual way of charging his customers: He lets them decide their own fare. Most of them give him cash, and he's hasn't been underpaid yet, but he has also received a $10 supermarket card and a musician's own CD.

WOW!

Fast trackers

Canadian adventurer Garry Sowerby and two British co-drivers drove 18,344 miles around the world in 1997, in a record time of just over 21 days.

CUT ABOVE THE REST

Brad Hauter from Indiana has traveled across the U.S.A. on a lawn mower! He journeyed over 5,600 miles from San Francisco to New York on a specially adapted mower as part of the Keep America Beautiful campaign in 2003. His mower reached speeds of 25 mph and Brad drove for 79 days and raised $150,000 for the campaign—and managed to mow 40 lawns along the way!

Long-distance love

It isn't easy to see your loved ones when you're a pilot, but Donna Clark travels over 16,600 miles a month to see her husband. Donna works as a U.S. pilot but her husband Bryan Clark is a hotel manager in Scotland, so Donna has to make the 8,318-mile round trip from Cleveland, Ohio, to see him using planes, trains, buses, cars, and ferries—and she does it twice a month!

Drive-through "I do"

As part of a car rally in Vasteras, Sweden, in July 2008, 50 couples had drive-in weddings. Ten priests from the Church of Sweden performed the 50 ceremonies, lasting 7 minutes each, alongside a procession of cars built in the 1950s and 60s.

Harrod Blank drives a van that is covered with over 2,000 cameras. He can operate them while he's driving to take surprise photos of passersby.

SELLING LIKE HOT CAKES

A cake created by bakers to advertise Skoda cars used 180 eggs, 125 jars of jelly, and 220 pounds of sugar. The cake was a full-sized car with

CHOCOLATE FROSTED TIRES,

aerial and wipers made of licorice, fondant icing paintwork, chocolate radiator grilles, and rear lights made of jello. Even the engine was cooked to perfection, but instead of oil, it was filled with syrup.

Re-cycling

Design student Phil Bridge from Stockport, England, has created a full-size bicycle made of cardboard! It's not just any cardboard: It is a strong, sturdy, waterproof card called Hexacomb, but it is still recyclable, still cheap (about $23 for the whole bike) and when the cardboard components wear out, the tires and chain can be refitted onto a new frame. Phil's idea is that the bike will be left alone by thieves, who won't want to steal something that seems so worthless.

Police raided a woman's home in Berlin, Germany, in 2004, and found piles and piles of stolen bicycles: 78 altogether.

Rocket man

U.S. Air Force Captain Chuck Yeager was the first man to fly faster than the speed of sound. In 1947, he piloted the Bell X-1 and reached

807 MPH!

Stan Barrett was the first to break the sound barrier in a car, reaching 739 mph in 1979, in his jet powered Budweiser Rocket Car.

I  Rolls-Royce

Graham Crossley of Sheffield, England, is so in love with Rolls-Royce cars that he even washes them for free, just to get close to them. He has been passionate about the top-notch cars for over 30 years and has more than 2,500 photos of them—but can't take one for a spin because he doesn't drive!

Former U.S. President Franklin D. Roosevelt refused to travel on the 13th of the month, because he was so superstitious.

Fuel saving

John and Helen Taylor of Melbourne, Australia, have driven right around the world on less than 24 tanks of fuel. They traveled at a leisurely pace to keep down fuel consumption, but still took only 78 days to cover the 18,100 miles in their VW Golf.

Italy's narrowest street is only 19.5 inches wide and is called "woman-kisser lane."

PICK A CAR, ANY CAR

This amazing building is 20 stories high and is full of hundreds of new cars waiting for collection. Drivers arrive at Volkswagen's Autostadt theme park in Wolfsburg, Germany, claim their new car, and wait for it to be lowered from its place in the tower—pretty much like waiting for candy from a vending machine, except your new vehicle isn't dropped from a dizzy height to pick out of a drawer at the bottom!

Taxi!

Archeologists in Rome, Italy, have found
remains of a carriage that is

2,000 YEARS OLD.

The carriage was pulled by horses and
carried fare-paying passengers. The fare was
calculated by a meter that dropped pebbles
into a container as the wheels turned. The more
pebbles, the higher the amount to be paid.

Ripley's
BIKES WITH ATTITUDE

When cyclists were asked for the worst things about being on two
wheels, they had several complaints, which were all taken into account
by ilovemybike.co.uk to design the ultimate bike. The result is the

A ski to glide through the snow...

a caterpillar track to smooth out
potholes...

Richard Hanner from Hellertown, Pennsylvania, drives around his hometown in an F-15 fighter jet! Not a real one, obviously: He has built a car that looks like the American jet plane. Inspired by his Uncle Joe, who was stationed on an aircraft carrier in the Navy, it cost nearly $10,000 and took 18 months to make. Known as the "Jet Trike" Is comes complete with cockpit, wings, tail... and three wheels.

Jewgenij Kuschnow balanced on his head for 15 minutes in Munich, Germany, in 2006–on top of a moving car!

B.O.N.D. (Built of Notorious Deterrents) bicycle, with enough gadgets to make even the super-spy happy. The B.O.N.D. has lots of gadgets, including a flame thrower to keep motorists at a safe distance, a caterpillar track to smooth out potholes, and even an ejector seat to get rid of thieves.

two flame throwing handlebars...

and an ejector seat!

Plucky pilot

Jamaican-born pilot Barrington Irving wants to be an inspiration for young people. Aged only 23, he flew solo around the world in three months, overcoming 100-mph winds, as well as monsoons, sandstorms, snowstorms, and freezing fog. He named his single-engine plane "Inspiration" as a message to others.

It has been calculated that in 2008, all the vehicles in the U.S. traveled nearly 2,922 BILLION miles—the same as driving to Pluto and back 390 times.

There are over a billion bicycles in the world-that's true pedal power!

PUSHY PASSENGERS

Traveling by plane is meant to be laid back. Simply board, stow your luggage overhead, and wait for takeoff, in-flight entertainment, and a smooth touch down. That all seemed to be the case for passengers flying to

ZHENGZHOU IN CHINA

in September 2008, until the plane broke down after landing. Airport staff couldn't move the jet off the runway and had to ask the passengers to help push the plane half a mile to safety, taking two hours!

IN THE HOT SEAT

Office workers in Bad Koenig-Zell, Germany, took part
in the first German Office Chair Racing Championship
in April 2008. Some of them just enjoyed
the experience of

ZOOMING ALONG THE STREETS

instead of being stuck behind a desk. Others dressed
in fancy dress for even more fun, while certain
competitive types put on safety gear, feeling the
need for speed.

Ripley's
FIRE! FIRE!

A cyclist from Poland was zooming along so fast on his bicycle that he set himself on fire!

He was pedaling furiously when he smelled burning.

Looking around, he noticed his pants were in flames—probably caused by the friction between his clothes as he pedaled.

63

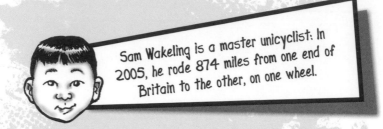

Sam Wakeling is a master unicyclist. In 2005, he rode 874 miles from one end of Britain to the other, on one wheel.

♪ KARAOKE CAB ♪

Passengers in Fan Xiaomning's taxi cab can sing along as they travel. The driver from Changchun, Jilin, China, has customized his cab with speakers, an amp, media players, LCD screens, and a microphone to make traveling much more fun.

Ripley's
PONY RIDE

Yes, you have just seen a horse in the back of a car. It was the only way the farmer could transport it, after buying the animal at an auction in Warsaw, Poland.

Going, going, gone!

Squeeeeeeeze!

He had to remove the back seats and strap them to the roof so the foal could fit for the 150-mile journey back to his farm. His car broke down on the way, so the police stepped in and found a better way to transport the poor creature.

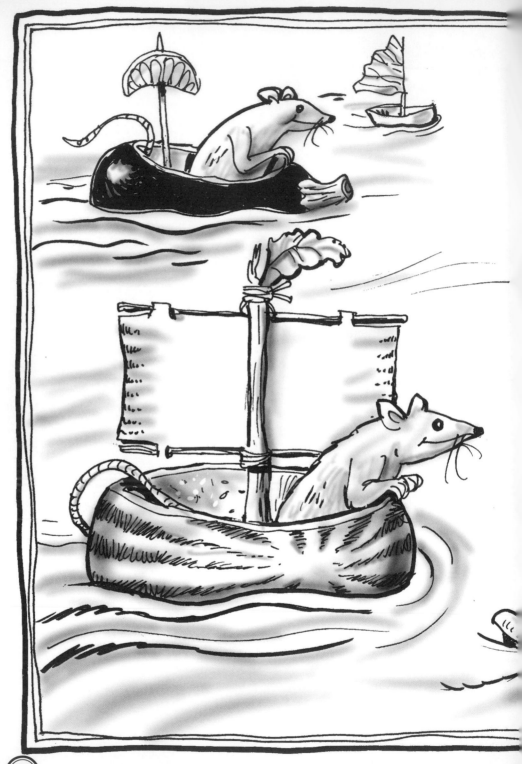

CRUNCHY CRUISERS

The people of Eyemouth in Scotland launched their lunch into the ocean for an edible boat race in 2008. Competitors had to design and build a boat made from foodstuffs; the pieces even had to be held together with candy laces and spaghetti strands. Melon-skin boats were super-seaworthy, but were disqualified for not being entirely edible.

TUNING THE ENGINE

He may not have had a boom box for his sound system, but J. Clark Cullom of Cincinnati, Ohio, could make music wherever he went... he simply strapped his piano to the back of his car! He traveled over 15,000 miles with his piano attached to the trunk, and must have made quite a din every time he hit a bump in the road.

A skateboard built in 2007 by Michigan students measures 31 feet long and 8 feet wide, and can hold 28 boarders at once.

TINY TOURER

The smallest street legal car in the world is the Peel P50, produced in the 1960s on the Isle of Man, Britain. The car is only 53 inches high and 39 inches wide: Big enough to fit just one adult. Its maximum speed is 38 mph and it has no reverse gear. However, it is so lightweight (just 130 pounds—the weight of an adult) that the driver can easily lift it and spin it on its back wheel to go in the opposite direction!

CABLE TRUCK

Liu Suozhu was high in the sky in 2007, when he drove his pickup along high wires, over 60 feet in the air! The truck driver from Korla City, China, carefully maneuvered his vehicle along 200 yards of parallel steel cables suspended between two hills, keeping on track for 15 minutes without veering off.

All four members of the Harriman family rode from Portland, Oregon, to Toledo, Ohio, in 1938—on the same motorcycle. They even took their dog, too!

Racing cart

Briton Edd China and American Rodney Rucker can carry a heap load of groceries between them. Each has built a giant motorized shopping cart that can be driven at speeds of up to

60 MPH!

Edd's cart stands over 11 feet high and is powered by a 600cc motorbike engine hidden in a large shopping bag. Rodney's cart towers 16 feet in the air and has seats for eight people!

Panic!

An unfortunate pilot who went to the toilet
during his flight found himself

LOCKED OUT OF HIS OWN COCKPIT!

Things could have got very tricky, as there was only half
an hour left of the 2006 flight from Ottawa to Winnipeg.
The pilot had to bang on the door for ten minutes
until his crew could let him in, by taking the faulty
door off its hinges.

Eau Claire's car
wash in Wisconsin
is shaped exactly
like a cruise ship! It
even has two smoke
stacks on top like
the real thing.

Coach party

Buses are more than just transport for some people:
They're an obsession. So much so that a group has formed
in Sao Paolo, Brazil, calling themselves the Bus Worshipers
Club. They meet to talk about, watch, and photograph
buses and their passengers, and are planning a grand bus
tour from Chile to Alaska. Tickets, please!

BED-RIDDEN

Is this the height of laziness? Englishman Edd China drives a four-poster bed, which is welded to a 1,600cc VW engine. The vehicle is legal on the roads, and Edd even takes tourists on

SIGHT-SEEING TRIPS

of London on board his bed. Edd loves crazy creations, and has also made motorized sheds, bathtubs, and a sofa complete with TV table to travel around in comfort.

Breathe in!

Stunt driver Dave Ackland from Devon, England, is a master of "car skiing:" a precision move that involves tipping a car on two wheels to squeeze through a narrow gap, just like James Bond. In March 2008, he maneuvered a Vauxhall Viva between columns of boxes just 6½ feet apart, only 2 feet more than the car itself measured.

Andorra, a tiny country in the European Pyrenees mountains, has no airports, sea ports, or trains.

UPSIDE DOWN

Lieutenant Tito Falconi flew 250 miles on August 27, 1933—upside down! The pilot from the Italian Air Force traveled the whole way from St. Louis, Missouri, to Joilet, Illinois—a journey of just over three hours the wrong way up in the sky.

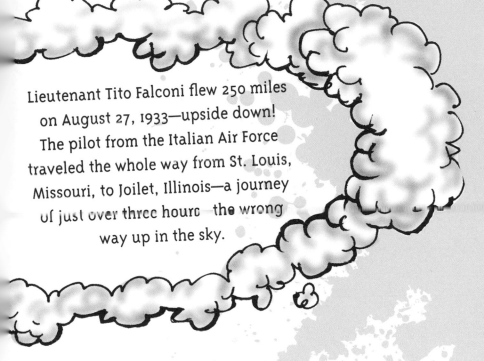

CAR CRUNCHER

Robosaurus is a force to be reckoned with! The metal monster stands 40 feet high and shoots flames 20 feet into the air, so stay well back! The mechanical dino crushes cars in its claws, and bites them in half with its huge teeth. The ravenous robot is controlled from inside its head by two people, but when it's time to go home, it folds right down into a standard-sized trailer to be towed along the highway.

LOONY LOAD

A trike is a great way to get about—it's eco-friendly, good exercise, cheap to run, and less wobbly than a two-wheeler. One thing it's not so good at is

LARGE LOADS

which is why a man in Anhul Province, China, got cautioned by the police as he cycled home with the best part of a whole car on the back of his bike!

FASTER, FASTER...

Waiting for a train
Gopal Dey of Howrah owns a train ticket for a journey to be made on June 28, 2073. Gopal, from Howrah, West Bengal, India, bought it in 1973 and is going to hand it down to his grandson.

Weak excuse
In Norway, a 79-year-old woman was declared too weak to drive, so had her license refused. How did they test her strength? She had to arm-wrestle her doctor!

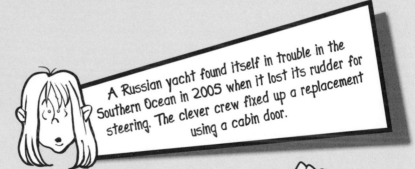

A Russian yacht found itself in trouble in the Southern Ocean in 2005 when it lost its rudder for steering. The clever crew fixed up a replacement using a cabin door.

INCREDIBLE!

The Vikings are coming!
An 11th-century Viking ship that sank near Copenhagen, Denmark, in 1072, has been excavated and in 2007 a recreation of it sailed 1,000 nautical miles from Denmark to Dublin, Ireland. The *Sea Stallion* is 100 feet long and made from the wood of 300 oak trees. It takes 60 oarsmen, or can use giant sails to propel it along at high speeds.

Driving like the wind

Imagine the surprise of the driver in Yanbian City, Jilin Province, China, as he drove round a corner and got blown into the air! A gust of wind lifted the car off its wheels and then high enough to hit the roof of a house, where it came to rest, the right way up.

The "cynosphere," an invention from 1875, is a tricycle powered by two dogs running inside the back wheels!

Whatever floats your boat

Students at the University of Nevada have made an eight-man canoe out of cement—and it actually floats!

Feeling flashy

In June 2008, New Zealand was hit by amazing electrical storms, with nearly 15,000 lightning strikes in 24 hours. During those storms, four airplanes were struck; one of them was a Lan Chile Airbus that managed to land safely in Auckland, despite having a hole the size of a dinner plate in its bodywork from one lightning blast.

Fuel gets more expensive every year—except for Abraham Noe-Hays, who uses free waste from restaurants! He has converted his 1989 VW Jetta to run on vegetable oil. Now, instead of finding a gas station, he pulls in to a fast-food outlet, hooks up to their fryer-fat dumpster, and fills up for free. Even better, he's not just saving money, but he's helping to save the planet by reusing resources and steering clear of fossil fuels.

HEAVY LOAD

No one can tell how sturdy this bicycle will be when fully loaded: But it certainly looks unbalanced! The three-wheeled, lightweight bike is carrying Styrofoam for recycling in Shanghai, China. Who knows if he made it safely or toppled over all that recycling?!

In August 2004, O.P. Sharma drove a motorbike through the busy streets of Patna, India, as part of his magic act: He was wearing a black bag over his head for the dangerous stunt.

DIVING DRIVING

How cool would it be to have a James Bond-style car that goes underwater? Now you can! The sQuba drives along roads like a sports car, but can dive down and "fly" through the water like a manta ray. The driver and passengers breathe air from tanks, like a scuba diver, as the car is open-topped to make it easy to escape in an emergency, and to keep the car light enough to drive on dry land.

Scuba diving dog Shadow goes on underwater adventures with his owner Dwane Folsom in his own special diving suit.

83

STREEEEEEEEEEETCH LIMO

A stretch limo is a sight to see, with room for up to

20 PASSENGERS INSIDE!

Imagine how it feels to travel in this 1980 Cadillac: The longest car ever built. It is 100 feet long and needs 26 wheels to support its full length. Inside there is a king-size waterbed and a swimming pool, and there's a helipad on the back!

AHHHH!

SPLASH!

Freaky Formula 1

Every year, entrants gather in the streets of Valentigney, France, to take part in the pedal-powered Grand Prix. Winning doesn't just require speed, but style, as each car and competitor must dress up. Previous entries have included a witch driving a pumpkin car, and a monkey at the wheel of a banana.

Budget airline

Bahadur Chand Gupta offers the ride of a lifetime—kind of. He charges $4 for people to board his plane, buckle themselves in, and watch safety demonstrations while being waited on by flight attendants. His Airbus 300 never leaves its parking space in Delhi, India, as it has only one wing, but his passengers are people who can't afford to fly and just want to see what it would be like.

Jumbo jets carry so much fuel that one tank could power a normal car FOUR times around the world.

Rapper attention

David Holmes, a U.S. flight attendant, delivers his safety instructions with style. His 80-second rap is just as informative as the standard speech, but includes lines like these:

BEFORE WE LEAVE, OUR ADVICE IS,

PUT AWAY YOUR ELECTRONIC DEVICES.

FASTEN YOUR SEAT BELT, THEN PUT YOUR TRAYS UP,

PRESS THE BUTTON AND MAKE THE SEAT BELT RAISE UP.

Square dancing is a common pastime across the U.S.A. but in Iowa the farmers often do the dance driving their tractors! They sure need a big dance floor...

A NEED FOR SPEED

Street luge is a crazy sport: Racers take part on winding downhill slopes, lying on a board that is only a couple of inches off the ground. They reach dramatic speeds and can crash with drastic effects. That's not enough for Joel King of Sussex, England, who wanted to break the record for a powered street luge. His board was fitted with a kerosene-powered jet engine that rocketed him along at 114.7 mph—on a board that has no brakes!

A CLEAN GETAWAY

Police officers in China were horrified when they stopped a truck on the busy Jinyi expressway and found that the driver had been taking a shower on the move! The police noticed water coming out of the cab, so they pulled it over. The driver was wet through from a sprinkler over his head; his wife covered the truck's instruments with plastic to keep them dry as he drove.

Something's missing!

The amazing Uno is an electric bike that uses gyroscope technology to stay upright. It actually has two wheels, side by side, and is controlled totally by body movements. Its inventor is a teenager from Ontario, Canada, named Ben Gulak, who can ride the bike up to

25 MPH!

The more he leans forward, the faster the bike goes, and he has to lean sideways to steer.

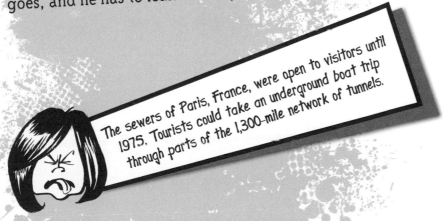

The sewers of Paris, France, were open to visitors until 1975. Tourists could take an underground boat trip through parts of the 1,300-mile network of tunnels.

Prize fighter

Cathie Llewellyn of Wintersville, Ohio, wanted a new car so badly that she lived in it for

20 DAYS.

Five people took part in the competition to win a PT Cruiser, but only two women lasted so long. Cathie was the final victor when 74-year-old Delores Milewsky had to quit for an illegal bathroom break.

Pieter de Hart, from the Netherlands, cycled almost 17 miles in 2002 facing backward while sitting on his bicycle's handlebars.

Any which way

The winner of the Mitsubishi Motors Fuso grand idea prize in 1996 was a car called the "Oval Runner." Instead of traditional round wheels, it had oval wheels, which allowed it to be driven in any direction, no matter which way it was facing.

In 2000, people spent more than a billion dollars just on taxi fares in the U.S.A.

DO YOU TAKE THIS... AIRPLANE?

Walking up the aisle was too boring for the marriage of Darren McWalters and Katie Hodgson in England. Instead, they took to the air and held their wedding strapped on top of a pair of biplanes! The bride and groom's planes flew next to each other at

1,000 FEET

and their brave vicar, George Brigham, flew ahead to perform the ceremony.

Fair play

A man nicknamed Dutch Charley attempted to fly from the top of one of Coney Island's fairground rides,

50 FEET IN THE AIR.

His "plane" was a wicker basket with no engine, only wings operated by cords, while Charley pedaled to provide power. Not surprisingly, the plane didn't take off, just plummeted into the ocean where Charley was rescued by lifeguards.

RIPLEY'S— UP, UP, AND AWAY

Traffic jams are no longer a problem for owners of the Terrafugia Transition Flying Car.

The four-wheeler, devised in Massachusetts, has folding wings and a propeller at the back.

LONG FORMULA

It's true—you can travel up to 140 mph in a stretch-limo-style Formula-1 car! The racing car was built by Canadian inventor Michael Pettipas, and seats six passengers plus the driver. The car is 30 feet long and legal to drive on public highways, doing 0—60 in five seconds.

Driving home

Dan Scully has built his house in the shape of a car! It has lots of auto-accessories, but it doesn't actually move from its plot in New Hampshire. The architect loves cars so much that he designed a home using the bumper from a VW bus, and windows like headlights. Inside, the chairs are actual car seats and the bathroom tiles look like tires.

If it's stuck in traffic it takes only 15 seconds to unfold the wings, and within 30 seconds the car can be airborne.

It flies at up to 130 mph and can cover 700 miles. Back home, the 27-foot wings simply fold back up and the car fits into a normal garage. Neat!

DOUBLE VISION

Many of the crazy cars in this book are part of the Art Car movement, but they don't come much crazier than Dennis Clay's VW Beetle. Dennis, from Houston, Texas, calls his work of art

"MIRROR IMAGE"

as there is an identical VW Beetle welded upside down on top of the first one.

ICE SCREAM!

Passers-by could be forgiven for standing well back as a 2-ton ice-cream truck careened

OUT OF CONTROL

in Reelsville, Indiana. They would certainly have been shocked if they'd caught sight of the driver as it zoomed 215 feet down a hill and into a tree: The ice-cream truck had a nanny goat at the wheel!

Ripley's —— **Believe It or Not!** ®

Hugues Richard from France climbed the steps to the second floor of the Eiffel Tower, Paris, in record time—on a mountain bike! He took 19 minutes, in April 2002.

Guy Negre has invented a car that takes no fuel, but runs on compressed air. It can reach speeds of 70 mph!

A Mexican limousine company has converted a Boeing 727 jet plane into a limo! It can carry 50 people and travels up to 125 mph.

Millionaire Jussi Salonoja was given a speeding fine in Finland of over $200,000, calculated on the basis of his income.

The first person to fly coast-to-coast across the U.S.A. was Calbraith Perry Rodgers, in 1911.

The fastest a human being has ever traveled is 24,791 mph, the speed reached by the astronauts in Apollo 10.

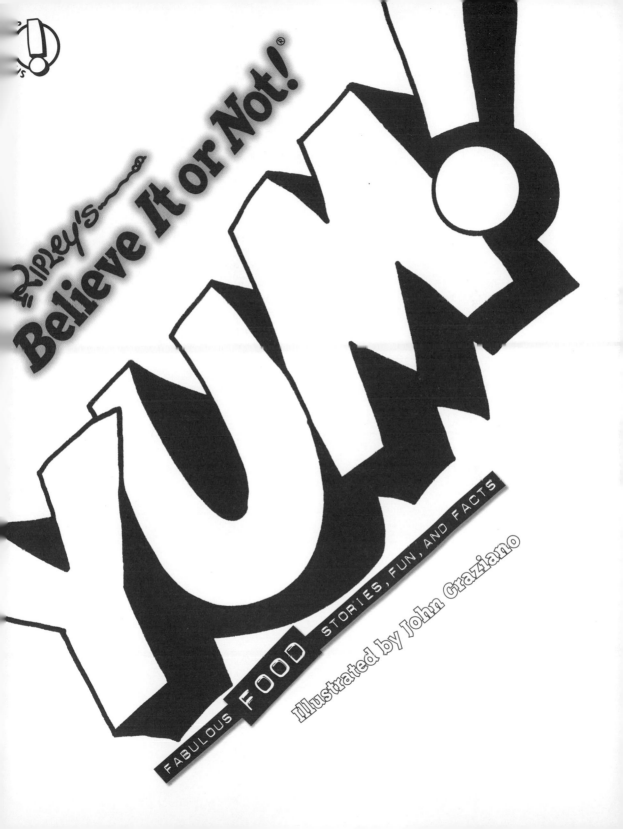

Ripley's— Believe It or Not!®

YUM!

FABULOUS FOOD STORIES, FUN, AND FACTS

Illustrated by John Graziano

PUBLISHING

Publishing Director Anne Marshall
Editorial Director Becky Miles
Art Director Sam South
Senior Designer Michelle Foster
Assistant Editor Charlotte Howell
Design Ark Creative
Reprographics Juice Creative

Ripley's——
Believe It or Not!®

YUM!

FABULOUS FOOD   STORIES, FUN, AND FACTS

Illustrated by John Graziano

Go to www.ripleys.com/books for more amazing facts

YUM!

food

You won't believe the crazy food people eat when you dip inside this fun-packed book! Read about shark's fin flavored ice cream, the hospital-themed restaurant, and the most bizarre canned food, including a whole chicken—plus much more!

It's Ripley's Shout Outs!

INTRODUCING... JOHN GRAZIANO

John, Ripley's very own cartoonist, has drawn every cartoon in this wacky book of crazy stories about food.

A new Ripley's cartoon has been produced every day for the past 90 years by a dedicated Ripley's cartoonist. John is only the eighth person to take on this role. Amazingly, he got himself the job 25 years after sending his drawings to Ripley's as a teenager!

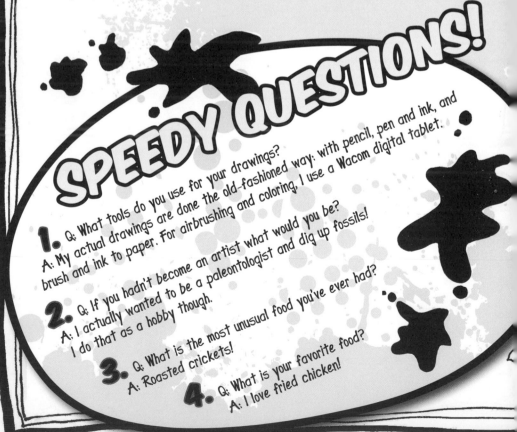

SPEEDY QUESTIONS!

1. Q: What tools do you use for your drawings?
A: My actual drawings are done the old-fashioned way; with pencil, pen and ink, and brush and ink to paper. For airbrushing and coloring, I use a Wacom digital tablet.

2. Q: If you hadn't become an artist what would you be?
A: I actually wanted to be a paleontologist and dig up fossils! I do that as a hobby though.

3. Q: What is the most unusual food you've ever had?
A: Roasted crickets!

4. Q: What is your favorite food?
A: I love fried chicken!

How to cook tarantulas

Where? In Skuon, Cambodia!
First, find a tarantula that's been specially bred in
holes in the ground. Then, fry it until the legs are stiff
and the abdomen is not too runny. You thus have
a crisp exterior, with a soft center, and
it's said to taste like chicken.
Now you know!

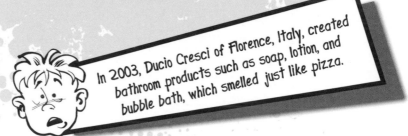

In 2003, Ducio Cresci of Florence, Italy, created
bathroom products such as soap, lotion, and
bubble bath, which smelled just like pizza.

Too hot to handle

Fact. Bhut Jolakia is the hottest chili on the planet. It is
one hundred times more fiery than the Jalapeno pepper
and has half the strength of

WEAPON-GRADE PEPPER SPRAY!

One bite would make most of us cry and burn our
stomach inside. So it's a mystery how a two-year-old boy
in Assam, India, is addicted to Bhut Jolakia chilies,
eating 50 in three hours without ill effects. He's
been devouring them since he was eight months old.

PULLING A FAST ONE

Joey Chestnut of San Jose, California, doesn't hang about when he's eating. He managed 103 Krystal burgers in just eight minutes in Chattanooga, Tennessee, in October 2007—that's 13 every minute, or one every 4.6 seconds! On July 4, 2009, he wolfed down 68 hot dogs in 10 minutes. His technique was to grab two hot dogs at a time and swallow them with the minimum of chews.

SODA MOUNTAIN

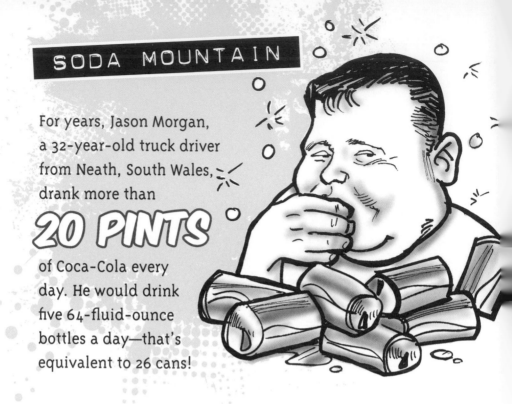

For years, Jason Morgan, a 32-year-old truck driver from Neath, South Wales, drank more than

20 PINTS

of Coca-Cola every day. He would drink five 64-fluid-ounce bottles a day—that's equivalent to 26 cans!

Fowl food

Les and Beryl Lailey of Manchester, England, celebrated their wedding anniversary in 2006 by eating a can of chicken given to them

50 YEARS EARLIER!

The can was part of a wedding gift hamper and they'd kept it as a souvenir of their happy day, promising not to eat it until their Golden Anniversary. When they finally opened the can, the chicken tasted as good as new, and they had it with some potatoes and vegetables.

DON'T SCOFF

"The Russian Giant," Fyodor Makhnov, born in 1878, was a big eater to say the least. His breakfast consisted of 20 eggs and eight loaves of bread. For lunch, he had 5 pounds of meat and 2 pounds of potatoes, then in the evening he ate 5 pounds of meat, three loaves, and some fruit, followed by a late-night snack of 15 eggs with another loaf. Well, he was 7 foot 10 inches tall, although some people insist he was as much as 9 foot 3 inches.

INCREDIBLE EDIBLES

All is not what it first seems in photographer Carl Warner's beautiful landscape pictures. The artworks have a secret ingredient—food! He makes forest scenes from broccoli, clouds from cauliflower or mozzarella cheese, mountains from bread, and buildings from Parmesan cheese. In other scenes, a little fishing boat, on close inspection, turns out to be a pea pod, resting on a sea of smoked salmon!

CRUNCH TIME

Where the wind blows
Cheekily, West Bromwich, England, has been labeled the U.K.'s Windy City, after a survey revealed its inhabitants to be the country's biggest fans of baked beans!

Breath of fresh air?
Don't go down to Garlic's Restaurant in London, Ontario, Canada, if you're on a first date or just don't like the reek of garlic. The menu there contains such smelly offerings as garlic ice cream and garlic cloves dipped in chocolate, both of which can be washed down with alcoholic garlic martinis.

Far-out fruit
Paul Friday of Coloma, Michigan, grew a peach that weighed an incredible 30½ ounces.

AMAZING!

No fewer than 8,400 people ate corndogs at the same time at the Iowa State Fair in Des Moines in August 2008.

Preserve energy
Any pickle for sale in Boston, Massachusetts, must be able to bounce 4 inches when dropped from waist height.

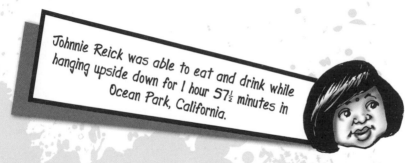

Johnnie Reick was able to eat and drink while hanging upside down for 1 hour 57½ minutes in Ocean Park, California.

Why not?

Chicago chocolatier Katrina Markoff makes some unusual combinations in her bars of candy, including curry and chocolate and chocolate with mushrooms. One of her culinary delights is Mo's Bacon Bar, which contains chunks of smoked bacon and milk chocolate. It sold out within 48 hours of going on sale at Selfridge's department store in London, England, in November 2008.

WOW!

Milking the benefits

Certain farmers in the Netherlands are pampering their dairy cows with massages and comfy mattresses to try to make them produce better-tasting milk! Nancy Vermeer's 80 cows are tucked up each night on 3 inches of soft rubber and sawdust, while some are lucky enough to get a waterbed.

NO WAY!

BUG BEARING

Students at the Iowa State University Entomology Club don't just study bugs, they eat them! They particularly like them with a Cajun sauce, covered in chocolate, or just dipped in jello.

Here's their recipe for banana worm bread

Banana Worm Bread

½ cup shortening • ¾ cup sugar • 2 bananas, mashed • 2 cups flour • 1 teaspoon soda • 1 teaspoon salt • ½ cup chopped nuts • 2 eggs • ¼ cup dry-roasted army worms

Directions

Mix together all ingredients. Bake in greased loaf pan at 350° F for about an hour.

Eat your heart out

In 2003, Barbara Jo from San José, California, made a gruesome cake based on the body's internal organs, complete with a white chocolate rib cage and different colored fruit juices that oozed out when each organ was cut. Iced veins were piped on and globs of gore added for that extra yuk value. The final touch—a glaze of corn syrup to create a gooey wet look.

One of the delights offered at a wild game restaurant in Guangzhou, southern China, is a plate of piping hot, cooked field rats.

Making waves

At his restaurant in Berkshire, England, chef Heston Blumenthal serves a dish that comes with an iPod Nano in a clamshell, so that customers can listen to the sea as they eat their seafood.

GECKO GETTER

It's not muesli or eggs that Mukesh Thakore
reaches for in the morning, rather it's a plate of
delicious lizards! He started eating the wriggly
reptiles at five years of age, when he found one
in the wild and popped it in his mouth out of
curiosity. In the 20 years since then, Thakore
reckons he's eaten more than 25,000 lizards—on a
good day, he can gobble up 25 live ones.

In the U.S.A.,
94 percent
of the
population
eat pizza.

Bucks fizz

Two hundred bottles of champagne sat happily on the
seabed off Finland for over 80 years, before
being sold off in 2008—for around

$300,000

a bottle! The 1907 champagne was on its way to the
Russian royal family when the ship that was carrying it
all sank. Anyone who fancies a sip should head off to the
Ritz-Carlton Hotel in Moscow, where bottles are being sold
to guests with expensive taste.

Chefs from a restaurant in Dohar, Qatar, dished up
a bowl of pasta measuring 20 feet long and 6 feet
6 inches wide and weighing 9,480 pounds.

Easter funny

What do you get if you crossed 50,000 chocolate
bars with 26 chocolate makers and masses of metal
scaffolding? The answer is an edible chocolate egg that
measures 27 feet 3 inches in height and 21 feet across,
weighing 4,299 pounds. It took eight days for such an
egg to be built around a wooden "shell" and be ready
to be displayed at Englewood Cliffs, New Jersey.

OFF ITS PERCH

Imagine the surprise of the Martinez-Guerra family in Campo Florido, Cuba, when their one-year-old hen laid a colossal egg weighing

6⅓ OUNCES.

That's nearly three times the normal weight of a hen's egg! It was so big that Titi the chicken couldn't sit on it.

Did you know that the first orange carrot was bred by Dutch farmers to honor their royal family, the House of Orange? Before that, most carrots were yellow, white, or purple.

Nosy man

Cheese-tester Nigel Pooley from Somerset, England, values his nose so much that he's insured it for $8 million. He uses his sensitive sense of smell to select more than 12,000 Cheddar cheeses every year.

BATHING BEAUTY

Why would anyone dress himself up as a full English breakfast? Well, that was exactly what Mark McGowan decided to do in November 2003 to show his support for English culture and food. He sat in a London shop window in a bath of baked beans, with two chips up his nose, and 48 sausages wrapped round his head! Mark's no stranger to strange behavior. Earlier that year, he pushed a peanut with his nose along 7 miles of London roads to the Prime Minister's front door.

Hot shot

While biting into a juicy hot dog in May 2004, Californian Olivia Chanes suddenly bit down on something hard. When she complained of a disgusting metallic taste in her mouth she popped to a hospital where doctors discovered that she'd swallowed a 0.4-inch bullet! What are the chances of that?

Vegetable seeds, launched into orbit to circle the Earth for two weeks in a rocket, produced supersize vegetables—9-inch chillies, 14-pound eggplants, and 200-pound pumpkins.

Grubby tale

Normally, if food looks moldy it gets thrown in the trash, right? Wrong. It's only when the Casu Marzu cheese from the island of Sardinia, Italy, is fully

INFESTED WITH MAGGOTS

that it's considered ready for eating! The maggot larvae of the cheese fly slop about in the cheese to give it the required moist texture, and then it's eaten, maggots and all. Groooss! When the maggots die, the cheese is unfit for human consumption.

PANCAKE RACE

The Fargo Kiwanis Club in North Dakota had a lot on its plate when it made nearly 35,000 pancakes in eight hours at its Pancake Karnival in February 2008. Every pancake was served up for eating, so it's no wonder the organizers of the event also had to provide 1,100 bottles of syrup for a topping.

FOOD FOR THOUGHT

Root of a problem

Unless it's prepared properly, cassava root, a common tropical food source, can poison a person as it contains cyanide.

NO!

Tall order

If Dutch Crown-Prince Willem-Alexander and Princess Maxima had wanted to cut the top layer of the bridal cake prepared for their wedding in February 2002, they might have been scrambling up a ladder. The cake rose to 59 feet above the town square in Ommen, the Netherlands, but the cool couple stayed firmly on the ground.

WOW!

Say cheese

For over 25 years, Dave Nunley from Cambridgeshire, England, has eaten nothing but grated Cheddar cheese. He munches his way through 238 pounds of it every year.

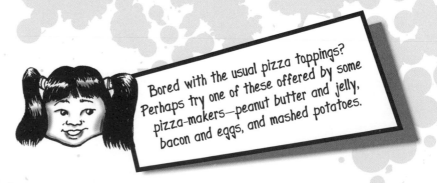

Bored with the usual pizza toppings? Perhaps try one of these offered by some pizza-makers—peanut butter and jelly, bacon and eggs, and mashed potatoes.

AWESOME!

Bling bagel

Would you pay $1,000 for a bagel? That was the price tag on one prepared by Frank Tujague, executive chef at the Westin New York Hotel, Times Square, in 2007. That's because it was topped with white truffle cream cheese and goji berry Riesling jelly with gold leaves. White truffle is the second most expensive food in the world—after premium caviar.

> Remember to try this succulent traditional dish when next in Tokyo—Taiwanese water bugs served on a bed of udon noodles.

Bumper bake

For the New York State Fair in 2004, Bruegger's Bakeries created a bagel that weighed in at 868 pounds, measured 6 feet across, and was 20 inches thick. It was boiled for 30 minutes and baked for nearly ten hours.

Crazy grazing

For many years, Gangaram, a man in Kanpur, India, has eaten more than 2 pounds of grass each day. He says he could live without food, but not without grass!

INCREDIBLE!

In 2009, it took 55 cooks 60 hours to bake a 2-ton cheesecake, which they cut into 20,000 slices.

Ripley's—➤ BEE=HAVE!

A Chinese man not only catches wasps, he also eats them! Zhong Zhisheng, from Shaoguan City, does not charge people for removing wasps nests from their homes, on condition that he is allowed to take the insects home and fry them. As pretty much no other animal eats wasps, he's tapping into a reliably constant food source.

SUNDAE BEST

When Mike Rogiani of Edmonton, Alberta, Canada,
says he's likes a big ice-cream sundae, he's
not kidding! In 1988, he spent

$7,000 ON INGREDIENTS

which included 63 different flavors of ice cream,
and then mixed them in an empty swimming pool.
The final, mouth-watering, creamy sundae
weighed a staggering 54,917 pounds.
That's a lot of licking.

NICE  BABY

It was hard to stay cool when you licked one of the ice creams that were being made by Japanese confectioners in 2002. The flavors were unusual to say the least, among them octopus, horseradish, shark's fin, garlic, potato and lettuce, whale and cactus, not to forget basashi vanilla, which contained chunks of raw horsemeat.

Big dipper

Just think of this. While you're watching football's most exciting game of the year on Superbowl Sunday, it's also a big day for the humble avocado. More than

43 MILLION POUNDS

of the green fruit are eaten during the game, most of it in the form of guacamole dip.

Rob Beaton of Asbury Park, New Jersey, used chopsticks to pick up and eat 78 single rice grains in 3 minutes, in November 2007.

A company in Taiwan makes dinnerware from wheat, so instead of washing up your plate at the end of a meal, you get to eat it!

GRAPE BALLS OF FIRE

The grapes on sale at The Kagaya Inn at Ishikawa, Japan, are the size of tennis balls! The tomato-colored Ruby Roman grapes, which have been under development since 1994, are so sought after that just one bunch, containing around 35 grapes, sold for

$910 IN AUGUST 2008.

$910

RIPLEY'S
BEAN THERE, DONE THAT

Fancy a cup of Kopi Luwak? That's Indonesian for Civet Cat Coffee and it's the most expensive coffee in the world! You can see what makes it so special here!

The civet cat spies ripe, yummy coffee beans...

...and feasts on them, choosing the best beans.

The civet cat then passes them out as partly digested pellets...

...just ready for the coffee growers to collect, wash them, partially roast them, and...

...Yum!

ONCE BITTEN...

When his stomach rumbles, Rakesh "Cobra" Narayan, of Moala, Fiji, will grab anything that takes his fancy—literally, anything. If shoes, grease, lizards, nuts and bolts, concrete, or even lawnmowers come his way, he'll eat them. His crazy cravings started when he was ten and he chewed some chicken wire. Afterward, he was still feeling a little bit peckish, so he popped a raw chicken into his mouth. At first, his mouth was cut by all the sharp objects, but now he suffers no side effects at all.

LAWNMOWERS

LIZARDS

HARD TO SWALLOW

World class

There's something for everyone in the International Burger, introduced in London, England, in 2008. Its ingredients come from seven different countries—check out the Japanese beef, pink Himalayan rock salt, Pata Negra ham from Spain, and Modena balsamic vinegar from Italy, all served up in an Iranian saffron and truffle bun.

WILD!

Deep breath

Spare a thought for the poor professional egg sniffer, whose job it was to break and smell between 7,000 and 11,000 eggs a day and sort good eggs from the bad.

Frog in your throat

A visit to a certain juice stall at the San Juan de Lurigancho marketplace in Lima, Peru, is not for the faint-hearted. You won't find freshly blended fruits there—rather, frog juice. Frogs are skinned and then blended to make a juice that is popular among some Peruvians, who believe it cures a range of common illnesses.

WOW!

Counting your chickens

Imagine eating chicken for breakfast, lunch, and dinner! Jan Csovary from Prievidza, Slovakia, does exactly that, consuming over 12,000 chickens since the early 1970s.

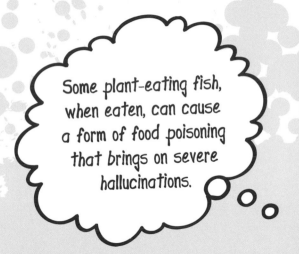

Some plant-eating fish, when eaten, can cause a form of food poisoning that brings on severe hallucinations.

Mega Macca

The same slab of ham has been on display at the Mecca restaurant in Raleigh, North Carolina, since 1937. The 25-pound ham was first acquired by the grandfather of the restaurant's current owner, Paul Dombalis, more than 70 years ago and has remained an uneaten favorite of customers ever since.

HUGE!

AMAZING!

Cut above the rest

If you find the regular butcher's fare boring, Theobald's Special Butcher shop in the Clerkenwell district of London, England, will sort you out. Customers can pick and choose from the range of highly exotic meats that the owner, Steve Ritchie, has to offer—zebra, camel, rattlesnake, ostrich, and kangaroo.

INCREDIBLE!

According to NASA scientists, the soil on Mars would be good enough to grow asparagus and turnips, but it isn't fertile enough for strawberries.

CANNED BE BAD

Next time you open a tin of something, check it doesn't contain some of the crazy canned food available around the world. If you've got adventurous taste buds, you could try tinned cheeseburgers, or canned cockroaches, fish mouths, or ants' eggs, or a whole chicken in a can, perhaps, complete with bones!

LARVA PALARVER

A restaurant in Germany enjoyed a rush of table bookings in 2005 after adding maggots to the menu. The Espitas restaurant in Dresden served up maggot ice cream, fried maggots with cactus and corn, and

MAGGOT

salads, washed down with maggot cocktails. The owner, Alexander Wolf said, "Most people were disgusted, but tried them out of curiosity and were amazed at how good the maggots tasted."

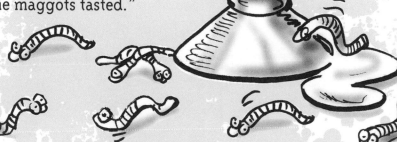

39

DEALS ON MEALS

Grub's up!

How many witchetty grubs would you need to eat a day in order to stay alive in the Australian outback? Answer—ten. The grubs, the larvae of the ghost moth, are highly nutritious, being rich in both calcium and iron. Some Australians eat them raw—others like them barbecued or made into a soup—and claim they taste of almonds.

Why not try the coffee-flavored chewing gum available in Japan that gives your breath that freshly brewed whiff?

INCREDIBLE!

Come on over!

Cooks in Caracas, Venezuela, made such a big pot of soup in September 2007 that they could have invited over 70,000 people to eat it. The 3,961-gallon soup contained 6,615 pounds of chicken, 4,410 pounds of beef, and literally tons and tons of vegetables.

AWESOME!

Bite of fresh air

Ever wondered why apples float in water? It's because they are 25 percent air.

Watch your manners!

There's no messing at Le Spirite Lounge in Montréal, Quebec. It's a vegan restaurant with a few strict rules, enforced by the owner who isn't afraid to shout at his guests. First, he insists that diners must finish their meal in order to get a dessert. Second, unless they finish their dessert, they cannot come back to the restaurant again.

Chicago food critic Fred E. Magel took his job seriously. He visited 46,000 restaurants in 60 countries over a period of 50 years.

No yolk

Michael Morris from Cornwall, England, was at home in April 2006, minding his own business and making an omelet for lunch. He cracked a big egg into a bowl and was amazed when a smaller egg fell out. Experts have described his egg-within-an-egg as really, really rare.

By hook or by cook

Just when one unlucky customer was enjoying a plate of fish at a restaurant in Shanghai, China, he suddenly got a fishhook stuck in his tongue. At first he thought it was just a bone, but then was rushed to the hospital where he had the fisherman's hook removed.

What Korean delicacy tastes best seasoned with lime or salt, or dipped in garlic butter? Answer—pan-fried grasshoppers, of course!

Coming in handy

No joke, on April 1, 1998, Burger King published a full-page advertisement in *USA Today* announcing the introduction to its menus of the

LEFT-HANDED WHOPPER

specially designed for the 32 million left-handed people in the U.S. The sandwich contained the usual lettuce, onions, pickles, mayonnaise, ketchup, and hamburger, but the ingredients were skewed to the left, so that left-handed eaters had fewer filling spills!

YUMMY GUMMI

Derek Lawson makes giant gummi bears at Popalop's Candy Shop in Raleigh, North Carolina. Each one weighs a massive 5 pounds and stands 9 inches tall, which is 1,400 times the size of an ordinary gummi bear. It takes nine hours to create each one and make it taste exactly like the original, smaller version.

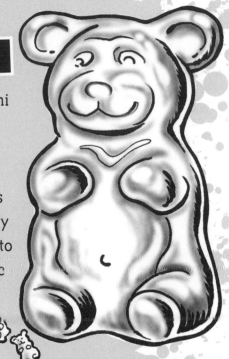

BEARING FRUIT

In 2008, 400 people from Swan Hill, Victoria, Australia, sliced and diced nectarines, plums, peaches, melons, and grapes to create a fruit salad that weighed a

WHOPPING 6¼ TONS.

It was loaded into a giant bowl and eaten the following day—Australia Day.

SPICY EYEWASH

Manuel Quiroz, a taxi driver from Mexico City, Mexico, can not only eat dozens of spicy chili peppers, but can rub them into his skin, and even squeeze the juice in his eyes! You've got to ask why he would do that? The answer, apparently, is that he feels no discomfort at all. He discovered this awesome talent when he was just seven years old.

A Belgian chocolate-maker created a room in Manhattan in 2008 that was entirely made from chocolate—including the walls, furniture, chandelier, fireplace, logs, and candles.

Try a flying visit to Connie's Airplane Bar, in Mississauga, Canada. You'll find yourself in a grounded airplane that's been turned into a restaurant.

MENU ON THE MENU

Even the menu at Molo restaurant in Chicago, Illinois, is edible! Chef Homaru Cantu loaded a modified ink-jet printer to use mixtures of fruits and vegetables and then printed tasty images loaded from the Internet onto edible sheets of soy bean and potato starch. Customers can flavor their soups by ripping up the menu and adding it to their food.

POTATO FUN

Every year the people of Clark, South Dakota, put a potato on a pedestal and spend a whole day celebrating the town's favorite vegetable.

In honor of the tasty tuber, a vast array of festivities are arranged—a dressing-the-potato competition that's enough to make Mr. Potato Head turn green with envy, as well as mashed-potato wrestling, in which combatants fight it out in a ring of mushy mash.

TOP TREATMENT

At a hospital-themed restaurant in Taipei, Taiwan, don't panic about your health if you find yourself drinking from the intravenous tubes that hang from the ceiling. Waitresses are dressed as nurses, crutches hang on the walls, a wheelchair is parked in the lobby, and the sign for the bathrooms is marked "Emergency room."

More than 300 accidents a year in Britain are said to be caused by bananas—most of them involve people slipping on skins.

Soda shower

Ever tried that trick where you drop a mint into a plastic bottle of cola and watch the drink explode crazily several feet into the air? Well,

1,360 STUDENTS

in Leuven, Belgium, donned plastic ponchos and did just that—all at the same time. The result was a massive, sticky, high-shooting fountain. So, remember, it's a trick for outside!

Up to one billion frogs are eaten by people around the world each year.

Burger birthright

What would life have been like without the very first burger? Three cheers for Louis Lassen and a moment in 1895 in his sandwich shop in New Haven, Connecticut. Louis didn't like to waste beef trimmings, so one day he ground them, grilled them, and served them between two slices of bread. The burger was born, and the rest is history. Phew!

Six chefs at a Tokyo hotel used 14,000 slices of bread to recreate a 10-foot-tall, 1,000-pound replica of the Japanese movie monster Godzilla.

Pizza whizz-er

Dennis Tran of Silver Springs, Maryland, is a fast foodie. Or rather he can make food fast—three large pizzas in just over

46 SECONDS

to be exact. That's an average of around 15 seconds per pizza. It's no small feat. He has to hand-stretch the fresh dough, apply pizza sauce, and top the three pizzas—one pepperoni, one mushroom, and one cheese.

BLIND DATE

Don't worry what you wear to a certain restaurant in London, England. No one can see you. Diners at Dans le Noir? eat in

TOTAL DARKNESS

the idea being that not being able to see what's on your plate heightens the senses and liberates the taste buds. Partly sighted or blind waiters serve the food and you're in big trouble if you take anything along that might shatter the blackness—cell phones are banned!

LIGHTS OUT!

INCREDIBLE EDIBLES

Whirling waiters

Talk about fast food! The Karne Garibaldi restaurant in Guadalajara, Mexico, claims to be able to serve a customer's food within 13 seconds of taking the order.

Rock or roll?

Just in case you were thinking of dropping round for a sandwich, it might be worth mentioning that Vivian Anderson from Cambridgeshire, England, has a bread roll that's about 90 years old! It was given to her grandfather in a ration pack while he was fighting during World War I, and it's been passed down through her family ever since.

WOW!

Fried sea horses are just some of the delicacies on sale at markets in Beijing, China.

Tea anyone?

Celestial Seasonings Tea made a massive tea bag weighing 106 pounds and showed it off in Toronto, Canada, in December 2007.

INCREDIBLE!

Gas line

Rudy Begonia's Belcher
is a super-fizzy soda made by a
Colorado company that guarantees the drink
will produce explosively loud belches!

Dishes of the day

Even if you're the fussiest of fussy eaters, you might just
have found something to pick at in the Las Vegas Hilton,
Nevada, in March 2006. A buffet was laid
out there, featuring no fewer than
510 different dishes—including
100 different salads,
40 varieties of soup, and
150 desserts.

Hammy performance

Archie McPhee, based in
Seattle, has produced a line of
dental floss with the flavor of crispy
fried bacon. The company already sells bacon-scented
air freshener, plus bacon-tasting mints and lip balm.

Hot hoofer

In just 5 minutes, Mark "The Human
Vacuum" Lyle ate 8 pounds 5 ounces
of chili at the Midwest Chili Eating
Championship in Canton, Ohio.

AMAZING!

Swedish astronaut Christer Fuglesang was the first to take dehydrated moose meat into space in December 2006.

AWESOME!

53

RED ALERT

Nicholas Huenefeld calls himself "The Human Ketchup Drinking Machine" and here's why. His personal bests are quaffing 13 fluid ounces of ketchup in 33 seconds, or

46 FLUID OUNCES

in 6 minutes! He started drinking the red stuff after a $5 bet at a restaurant. He now wants to increase his metabolism and his breathing rate, so he can slurp more quickly and intensely.

CHEESE... TASTIC!

In 16th-century Denmark, cheese was a form of currency. People paid their taxes with cheese!

Big Apple, big chow

In July 2009, when 39,000 baseball fans ate potato chips simultaneously in the middle of the second innings of a game between the New York Mets and the Cincinnati Reds at Citi Field, New York, the crunch could be heard all over the ground. Didn't their moms tell them to close their mouths when eating?

SLICKER LICKERS

Waggs Foods in North Yorkshire, England, has come up with a range of luxury ice creams—for dogs. Hungry hounds that need to cool off can lap at such flavors as Panting Peanut Mutter, Oaty Pawfection, and Chase Your Tail Cheesecake. The nice ices contain hidden dog biscuits, as well as Yucca extract to reduce the unpleasant smells from doggy wind!

THE BIG BANG

Imagine taking a bag of "this" popcorn into the movies—in 2009, hundreds of volunteers from Sac City, Iowa, used 1,500 pounds of popcorn, 2,400 pounds of sugar and 1,100 pounds of syrup to mix an enormous popcorn ball weighing around

5,000 POUNDS.

Sac City produces 5 million pounds of popcorn every year.

Bar bar black choc

Jane Marshall from Derbyshire, England, owns a chocolate bar that is 105 years old. It was made to celebrate King Edward VII's coronation in 1902 and was given to her by her grandfather when she was nine.

Hot chocolate

So you think you love chocolate, but do you think you love it enough to pay out money for a single chocolate made in Japan for Valentine's Day? To celebrate the the year 2006, it was encrusted with

2,600 DIAMONDS

putting up its value to 500 million Yen ($6 million). It was designed in the shape of the continent of Africa.

For over 40 years, Jiang Musheng of China has eaten live tree frogs and rats to ward off abdominal pains.

Flying frier

Jay Barr of Cape Coral, Florida, makes an hour-long, 150-mile flight to Kissimmee, Florida, ten times a year—just to buy hamburgers. He buys them in packs of 24 from the nearest Krystal fast-food restaurant. The Krystal company was so impressed by Mr. Barr's devotion to their burgers that it unveiled a hamburger box and a drink cup with his face and an airplane printed on them.

HEAD LINES

It wouldn't be surprising if Lodi, a restaurant in California, had the biggest collection of bald-headed customers in the world. That's because the restaurant's owner, Gary Arnold, charges people according to the amount of hair on their head. The hairiest pay most and totally bald people eat for free!

FANCY A LICK?

Everyone loves a Popsicle, but one with a wiggly worm in it sounds gross. Annie Munoz doesn't think so though. In June 2007, she launched her collection of Popsicles filled with grasshoppers and oatmeal worms in Panama City. This might even be good news for kids—with that addition of a little bit of protein, parents might be more keen to let their offspring have a Popsicle!

Pass them round

A British chocolatier made a box of chocolates in London's Leicester Square in 2008 that's never going to fit in your average Christmas stocking. It weighed 4,805 pounds, stood 16 feet 6 inches high, 11 feet 6 inches wide, and contained more than 222,000 chocolates.

SITTING PRETTY

Don't flush with embarrassment when you sit down at the toilet-themed restaurant Martun ("toilet" in Chinese), in Kaohsiung, China. Diners there perch on

TOILET SEATS

and the food arrives in bowls shaped like Western-styled toilets or Asian-style "squat pots." Even the food is designed to resemble manure, but thankfully only in appearance try the soft, chocolate cream whipped into a whirl and served in a potty.

GNAW JOKING

Cheese sleaze
In the 12th century, Blanche of Navarre thought that the way to win the heart of the French King Philippe Auguste was to send him 200 cheeses every year.

INCREDIBLE!

Whizzy fizzies
Jones Soda Co. really got the taste buds jangling with the range of sodas it came up with for Qwest Field, home of the Seattle Seahawks football team. Their new flavors tapped into some key features of the game but sounded disgusting all the same. Fancy a refreshing slug from a soft drink called Perspiration, Dirt, Sports Cream, or Natural Field Turf?

CRAZY!

In 1992, a 352-pound tuna sold at an auction in Japan for a whopping $69,273.30.

Corn dolly
In 1947, Virginia Winn from Mercedes, Texas, decorated an evening dress with 60,000 grains of corn, and then found it weighed 40 pounds!

NO WAY!

Every day since 1972, Don Gorske from Wisconsin, has eaten on average of two Big Macs. On July 19, 2004, he swallowed his 20,000th Big Mac.

Italian invasion

Guess how many pizzerias there are in the U.S.A. Answer—61,300, with over 9,000 in New York City alone.

Bizarre burrito

Some called the 2007 food festival in the Mexican town of Santiago de Anaya a gastronomic delight, others were less complimentary. Either way, it featured all sorts of flora and fauna in more than 1,000 dishes, such as delicious worm and armadillo burritos and a rather special rattlesnake meat taco.

WOW!

Hot cash

The workers responsible for grinding Dijon mustard were often given cash bonuses when the strong fumes from the mustard made their eyes water.

WHOA!!

Going bananas

The world's first banana pyramid was built in Madrid, Spain, using more than 6 tons of bananas.

Old favorites

Guess what archeologists unearthed in 2005 on an archeological site in Lajia, China? Treasure maybe? No, noodles reckoned to be about

4,000 YEARS OLD!

The only difference between them and modern noodles is that they were made from millet instead of wheat flour. They're thought to have been buried during a catastrophic flood.

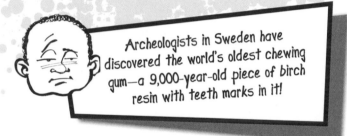

Archeologists in Sweden have discovered the world's oldest chewing gum—a 9,000-year-old piece of birch resin with teeth marks in it!

SWEET PICTURES

Australian artist Sid Chidiac's pictures are finger-licking good, because he paints with chocolate. Food dye and only the finest Belgian chocolate go on an edible canvas to create portraits of, among others, John F. Kennedy, Oprah Winfrey, and Abraham Lincoln. Each picture takes three days to finish and then has to be kept in cool conditions —and away from chocoholics!

RIPLEY's
THERE WAS AN OLD LADY...

1. An Israeli woman in 2003 was not only unfortunate enough to have...

2. ...a cockroach jump into her throat while she was brushing her teeth,

3. but when she tried to retrieve the insect from her throat with a fork,

4. she swallowed that, too. How unlucky can you be?!

65

TOMATO FORCE

Everyone saw red in Guiyang, China, in 2009, when hundreds of people hurled big, fat, squashy tomatoes at each other at an event organized by a local shopping mall. The fight was inspired by the famous

Tomatina festival, in Bunol, Spain, when 30,000 people turn up to pelt

the living daylights out of each other with tomatoes. In China, the

juicy battle required a massive haul of the ripe fruit weighing the same as 20 family cars and costing $15,000. Luckily, the shopping mall was at hand for new clothes.

Slippery customers

Feeling low? What you need is the new energy-boosting drink on sale in Japan—made from eels. The yellow, fizzy drink contains extracts from the heads and bones of eels, along with some fishy vitamins.

EXTRA TOPPINGS?

To celebrate the 859th anniversary of the founding of their city, pizza lovers in the Russian capital, Moscow, created a map made from pizza. Measuring almost

20 FEET IN DIAMETER

it featured sculptures of the Kremlin and other Moscow landmarks made from gooey cheese on the top.

A square or a hump?

Hurrah! Dubai-based Al Nassma has produced chocolates that are seriously low in fat and high in Vitamin C. Possibly the only off-putting part of the good news is that the chocolate's made from

CAMEL'S MILK.

The company has 3,000 camels, which produce enough milk to make 100 tons of chocolate a year.

American baseball fans go through 26 million hot dogs a year, enough to circle a baseball diamond 36,000 times.

Happy eater

Ten people toiled away for 300 hours building a giant chocolate billboard in London, England, but why is it no surprise that it took lucky passers-by just three hours to eat the lot! The sign measured

14½ FEET BY 9½ FEET

and was made from ten chocolate bunnies, 72 large Easter eggs, and 128 chocolate panels, each of which weighed more than 4 pounds.

In 2007, more than 1.5 million people logged on to an Internet site to watch the live filming of a Cheddar cheese slowly maturing in Somerset, England.

Crunchy critter

All scorpions should keep out of the way of Hasip Kaya of Turkey, who can't stop eating them live. He's been feasting on the nippy nippers since childhood and is so addicted to them that friends and family in his village are constantly looking under rocks to find him fresh supplies.

INSIDE STORY

Watch your behavior in Qiufan restaurant in Wuhan, China, or you might never leave. The whole vibe there is that of a jail. Customers enter through a big metal door and are greeted by staff wearing prison uniforms. Handcuffed, the guests are then led to their cell, which is complete with rusty iron bars and a sliding, lock-tight door.

Have your cake and hit it

What's one of the best ways to get rid of some pent-up anger? A good

FRUITCAKE BASHING

that's what! That's exactly what goes on every January at the Giant Fruitcake Toss, held in Manitou Springs Memorial Park in Colorado. Participants have a grand old time, swatting unwanted Christmas fruitcakes with

BASEBALL BATS

hitting them with golf clubs, flinging them from catapults, and hurling them from rooftops.

PET LOVE

If someone says your date looks like a bit of a dog, don't be offended. He or she might be! A restaurant in China encourages human customers to eat at the same table as their pets. Although the menu is primarily for animals, it also offers drinks and snacks for pet owners. The Paradise Pet Club in Shanghai disinfects its dishes three times a day.

Take your pampered pooch down to Dudley's Dog Bakery in Fort Myers, Florida, where Vickie Emanuele produces freshly made fancy gourmet treats and cakes—just for dogs.

MUNCH BUNCH

Needles and fins

A Japanese company performs relaxing acupuncture on each tuna fish about to be killed and eaten, in order to reduce the stress the fish suffers.

AWESOME!

Americans eat 251,770,000 pounds of pepperoni, their favorite pizza topping, every year.

Serpent supper

Neeranjan Bhaskar claims to have eaten not one, but 4,000 snakes, including deadly cobras! Strangely, Neeranjan says he's a vegetarian—apart from the snakes, that is. He ate his first snake at the age of seven and hunts for the slippery customers every morning on the banks of the Ghagra River near his home in India.

Egg-fried nice

Over 60,000 eggs went into the 6,510-pound omelet whisked up by the Lung Association of Brockville, Ontario, Canada, in 2002.

EGGSTRODINARY!

And swallow...

OK, so it's great to have a wide range of food to choose from, but there may be limits. Take the *baozi*, a traditional Chinese steamed bun. It's usually stuffed with a meat or vegetarian filling, but in one neighborhood of Beijing there's a third filler offered— chopped cardboard! The cardboard's softened in caustic soda and enhanced with pork flavoring before being added to the buns. Yum!

Greens shoot

If an average butter bean is about an inch long, the one grown by backyard gardener C.W. Forschner of Cleveland, Ohio, was truly exceptional. It measured 27½ inches in length and 20½ inches across.

More hen

The average meat-eater consumes 1,200 chickens during his or her lifetime— that's 3,970 pounds of chicken meat, the equivalent of eating a four-year-old elephant.

For 23 years, Mrs W. E. Updegraff of Vinita, Oklahoma, made 60 pies in just 45 minutes, every weekday. That's a total of 380,000 pies!

BED CRUMBS

Most moms warn never to eat in bed, but anyone who has always fancied doing just that should go to a restaurant, aptly called Duvet, in New York, where customers eat on king-size beds and the lighting is reading-light low. It's furnished with about 30 beds, pillows, and sheets, instead of tables, chairs, and tablecloths, and dinner is served on TV trays, while customers lounge about just as they please.

TOP TABLE

In May 2004, six friends, dressed in top hats and dinner suits, carried chairs, a table complete with starched white tablecloth, plates, cutlery, wine glasses, and even a candelabra up to

22,000 FEET

and sat down to a formal supper. As the snowy location was just 7,000 feet below the summit of the world's highest mountain, Everest, and the temperature touched minus 40°F, the drinks were already chilled.

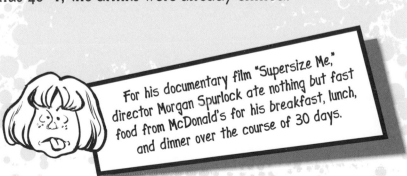

For his documentary film "Supersize Me," director Morgan Spurlock ate nothing but fast food from McDonald's for his breakfast, lunch, and dinner over the course of 30 days.

Eggs-actly right

Everyone's got an opinion on how many minutes you should boil an egg to produce the right consistency of yolk and white. Now, to settle any arguments, experts at the British Egg Information Service have found a way to achieve a perfectly cooked egg. As the egg starts to cook, a temperature-sensitive ink stamp on the shell turns black to show whether inside the egg is soft-, medium-, or hard-boiled. Sorted.

In less than 2 minutes in 1982, Ken Edwards of Cheshire, England, ate 12 live slugs, followed by two Brillo pads for dessert.

D'you wanna go large?

Like your fries? If so, stick close to Alan Williams of Hereford, England, who in February 2004 fried up more than 800 pounds of potatoes to produce a bag of French fries weighing over

400 POUNDS.

On top, he offered 50 pounds of salt and 30 gallons of vinegar to make them as tasty as possible. They must have been good—not one fry went uneaten.

SAND-WICH ANYONE?

Imagine if your weekly groceries included a massive bag of sand! That's the case for 80-year-old Ram Rati of Lucknow, India, who crunches her way through

1 LB OF SAND EVERY DAY.

She's been eating it before each meal for the last 40 years and says it helps her to fight old age and stomach problems.

Nutty as a fruitcake

Baking mad George D'Aubney spent three years building a 4-foot, inside-and-out replica of the famous London, England, landmark St. Paul's Cathedral. It came complete with lights, music, and moving parts—oh, and it was made primarily of fruitcake! "No one's eating it," assured George.

Mary Horton is addicted to sugar! On average, she eats 2 pounds of it every day.

Yummy money

In 2002, one of Britain's fanciest grocery stores, Fortnum & Mason, advertised for a chocolate taster, with a salary equal to $54,000 a year. To earn the pay, the taster had to travel the world sampling as much chocolate as possible. It's a tough job, but someone's got to do it..

COOKIE COOK-OUT

A giant chocolate-chip cookie, baked by the Immaculate Baking Company in 2003, weighed in at a staggering

40,000 POUNDS.

Displayed at Flat Rock, North Carolina, it took eight hours to bake, and required 30,000 eggs and a cookie sheet the size of a basketball court.

Cooking flat out

A monster focaccia bread was baked in the small town of Mottola in Italy, but no monsters turned up to eat it—just

40,000 SPECTATORS.

It covered an area of 4,840 square feet. That's nearly 1¼ tennis courts! The oven alone measured 4,840 square feet and the flat bread, when cooked, weighed 62,000 pounds.

In 2007, a huge calzone pizza, 19 feet 4 inches long and weighing more than 100 pounds, was cooked up by a restaurant in Madison, Wisconsin.

Good enough to eat

Why not sink your fangs into the Dracula dessert, complete with Crucifix biscuits, at the Vampire Café in Tokyo, Japan? Relax among the restaurant's blood-red velvet walls, the

MAKE-BELIEVE CORPSES,

skulls, spiders, crosses, and black coffins dripping with red candle wax. Then trot along home for a peaceful night's sleep—if you can!

A HEAD FOR FIGURES

Pastry chef Roland Winbeckler of Kent, Washington State, makes life-sized replicas of famous people from completely edible ingredients. His George Washington cake stood 6 feet 2 inches tall and weighed over 30 pounds. Other lookalikes he's made include Elvis, Cher, Marilyn Monroe, and the great explorer, Christopher Colombus.

MIGHTY MUNCHER

Introducing… an official pizza-eating world champion! Patrick "Deep Dish" Bertoletti from Chicago can devour 47 slices of 16-inch deep-dish pizza in 10 minutes, but his talents don't stop there. He can polish off 10 pounds of Key Lime Pie in 8 minutes, 275 pickled peppers in 10 minutes, and 3 pounds of bull's testicles in 10 minutes. Mmm! Despite regularly gulping down more than 10,000 calories in just a few minutes, Patrick is no heavyweight. At 6 foot 2 inches he weighs a slim-line 190 pounds.

PLAYING WITH FOOD

Vegetables are the only instruments in the Vienna Vegetable Orchestra. Founder Jorg Piringer plays a reed instrument called a gurkaphon, which is made from a hollowed-out cucumber, a green pepper, and a carrot. Other "Veggies" play carrot flutes, leek violins, and eggplant cymbals. After a concert, a chef turns the instruments into a vegetable soup that the audience and musicians all share.

ON A DIET

A retired couple from England have traveled 60 miles on the bus for a fish-and-chip lunch at their favorite seaside resort every day for the past ten years. Ermis and Androniki Nicholas have visited Weston-super-Mare, Somerset, over

2,600 TIMES

journeying 160,000 miles and spending over $30,000 on the fish and chips. Even though it's a pretty fatty food, they walk 6 miles around the resort after lunch and Mr. Nicholas has lost 85 pounds in weight as a result.

Going veggie

Brussels sprouts have that reputation for being, well, a bit windy, so it was worth standing upstream from Richard Townsend when he ate 37 sprouts in 60 seconds in December 2006. After his gigantic gobbling, Richard said he couldn't face another sprout for a few days, but then popped another in his mouth, saying,

"IT'S A SHAME TO WASTE THEM."

TEA FOR ALL!

In May 2009, Anne Tattershall from Devon, England, served up an enormous cream tea that featured a single scone weighing 99 pounds and measuring

3 FEET ACROSS.

It took four bakers—Nick, Amy, and Mary Lovering and Simon Clarke—to make the scone, which was filled with 20 pounds of jelly (that's about the same weight as a medium-sized car tire) and 35 pounds of clotted cream.

Check the ingredients in a certain Japanese sports drink said to aid tired muscles, and you'll find listed the saliva of Japan's giant hornets.

Small fry

Most of us would find finishing just one traditional British cooked breakfast a challenge, but the winner of the first All You Can Eat Breakfast Eating Championships held in London in 2007 managed 5½ breakfasts in only 12 minutes! Each breakfast consisted of a delicious pile of

EGGS BACON SAUSAGES MUSHROOMS AND CROISSANTS

Shai Pariente went to great lengths to win an iPod. He clinched first prize in a 2004 competition in New York City by eating 13 oven-roasted cockroaches.

THEY'RE NOT NOODLES!

Mark Hogg from Louisville, Kentucky, can eat 94
worms in just 30 seconds! In fact, he loves the chewy
crawlers so much that he once buried himself in
them right up to his chin. Standing in a container,
arms pinned down, with 10,000 worms squirming all
around him, Matt happily slurped and snacked
for an hour—to eat his way out.

ROBO-CHEFS

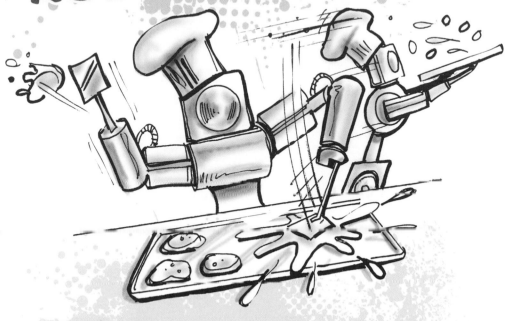

The only human involvement in the kitchen at a restaurant in China is the cutting up of the ingredients that go into the food. Robot chefs do the cooking. Hundreds of recipes for traditional Chinese dishes have been stored in the databases of the computers that control the movements of the two robots at the I Robot restaurant in Nanning, Guangxi Province.

So hard is Blue Vinny cheese that a whole cheese wheel was once used as a temporary wheel replacement on a train.

Here come the brides

When Chidi and Innocent Ogbuta of Dallas, Texas, renewed their wedding vows, it wasn't clear if the bridegroom would

SAY "I DO"

to the right girl. That's because they were joined by a 5-foot wedding cake that was an identical, life-sized model of the bride. The

$6,000, 400-POUND

butterscotch cake took five weeks to make, and contained 2 gallons of Amaretto liqueur, 50 pounds of sugar, and 200 eggs.

U.S. First Lady Eleanor Roosevelt used to eat three chocolate-covered garlic balls every morning. She believed it improved her memory, but it did nothing for her breath!

Hot bath

A Japanese health spa is offering the unusual specialty of a communal curry bath to its customers. Those who are brave enough to try it, step into the green soupy bath that contains a blend of curry spices, including turmeric and red pepper. It's said to improve blood flow, help boost metabolism, and produce beautiful skin.

HOT MEAL

When Iceland's Fimmvörðuháls volcano erupted in April 2010, Reykjavik chef Fridgeir Eiriksson stayed cool in the heat. Making the most of the situation, he cooked soup, flaming lobster, monkfish, and shallots using the volcano's 3,908 °F lava as an oven. Two customers paid $1,000 to enjoy this special champagne dinner on the bubbling volcano.

KIDS RULE!

At the Kinderkookkafe, a café near a play park in Amsterdam, the Netherlands, kids get to be in charge. All the food is cooked and served by children, who then bring the bill and wash up. Adults aren't even allowed to eat there unless they have been invited by a child.

RIPLEY'S
MIDNIGHT FEAST

When one burglar raided houses in Seattle in August 2004, he ignored all jewelry and went for the fridges.

He stole six shrimp kebabs, 12 mini corndogs, half a pack of cooked meat, 12 balls of cookie dough...

...handfuls of candies, a box of Creamsicles, two fruit drinks, and a glass of milk.

In another raid, he thawed and fried steaks and ate them while watching TV!

95

RIPLEY's
DID YOU KNOW???

A hamburger made by Denny's Beer Barrel Pub in Clearfield, Pennsylvania, on June 1, 2004, weighed 11 pounds. Would that be "to go"?

Every election day in Eyrie, Pennsylvania, Democrats at the Polish Falcons Club eat duck blood soup!

In just over one minute in 1978, Canadian Pat Donahue ate 91 pickled onions.

Americans eat about 350 slices of pizza per second, that's about 100 acres of pizza each day.

Gelatin, the thickener used in many foods, such as ice cream and cereal, is made from animal skins, hooves, and skeletons.

Danny Partner from Los Angeles, California, loved iceberg lettuces covered in chocolate sauce so much that he ate 12 of them every day.

Ripley's—
Believe It or Not!®

GAME!

MAD SPORTS STORIES, FUN, AND FACTS

Illustrated by John Graziano

PUBLISHING

Publishing Director Anne Marshall

Editorial Director Becky Miles

Art Director Sam South

Senior Designer Michelle Foster

Assistant Editor Charlotte Howell

Design Ark Creative

Reprographics Juice Creative

Ripley's—
Believe It or Not!®

GAME!

MAD SPORTS STORIES, FUN, AND FACTS

Illustrated by John Graziano

GAME!

Sports

You won't believe the crazy sports stories you're about to read when you dive inside this fun-packed book! Check out tales of snail spitting, ostrich racing, gravy wrestling, and yak skiing, plus many more! **It's Ripley's Shout Outs!**

INTRODUCING... JOHN GRAZIANO

John, Ripley's very own cartoonist, has drawn every cartoon in this wacky book of crazy sports stories.

A new Ripley's cartoon has been produced every day for the past 90 years by a dedicated Ripley's cartoonist. John is only the eighth person to take on this role. Amazingly, he got himself the job 25 years after sending his drawings to Ripley's as a teenager!

SPEEDY QUESTIONS!

1. Q: What tools do you use for your drawings?
A: My actual drawings are done the old-fashioned way with pencil, pen and ink, and brush and ink to paper. For airbrushing and coloring I use a Wacom digital tablet.

2. Q: If you hadn't become an artist what would you be?
A: I actually wanted to be a paleontologist and dig up fossils! I do that as a hobby though.

3. Q: Which of the sports stories is your favorite?
A: I am partial to the camel racing!

4. Q: What sport would you like to try?
A: Definitely the pogo stick!

World at his feet

Perhaps the greatest soccer player of all time, Pelé scored

1,281 GOOOOALS

in his career—more than any other professional player. The Brazilian helped his country win three World Cups, and scored the opening goal in the 1970 World Cup Final, when Brazil beat Italy 4-1.

America's Edwin Moses won gold medals in the 400-meter hurdles at the 1976 and 1984 Olympics. He was not beaten in 122 races in a row between 1977 and 1987.

Over a barrel

Curiously, Bottle Kicking competitions in Leicestershire, England, involve neither bottles nor kicking, but have been held on Easter Monday since 1771. Rival villagers from Hallaton and Medbourne fight over three small beer barrels and try to drag and push them over their opponent's line. The goal lines are two streams that lie a mile apart, and the contest is tough and hard—it can last for hours!

Ripley's
WIPE YOUR TIRES!

Competitors in the Down the Hill bike race in Taxco, Mexico, hurtle down the village's steep steps...

...and whizz through the narrow passageways of the town at very fast speeds.

At one point in the race, they even cycle through a house! They go in through one door...

...ride down a flight of stairs, and exit through another door, leaving muddy tire marks behind!

11

Dead funny

Every year in Manitou Springs, Colorado, around 40 teams race coffins with a living female inside. The race is held in memory of Emma Crawford, who died in 1890 and was buried on the top of Red Mountain, only to have her coffin slide down the canyon in 1929 after heavy rains!

During a single game on June 29, 2007, Brad Turney of Alexandria, Louisiana, played all nine positions for the minor league baseball team, the Alexandria Aces.

LONG-DISTANCE CALL

At the Cell Phone Throwing World Championships in Finland, competitors get to throw their phones around! One of the sport's top competitors is the U.K.'s Chris Hughff, who can

HURL A PHONE

an impressive 314 feet. First prize, not surprisingly, is a new phone.

Darts player Perry Prine, from Mentor, Ohio, threw

1,432 BULL'S-EYES

in 10 hours in March 1998. In that time, he fired 6,681 darts—that's 11 darts a minute, of which, on average, 2.39 were bull's-eyes. In the 10 hours he played, he reckoned he walked 3 miles to and from the dartboard!

In February 2009, Bulgarian grandmaster Kiril Georgiev played 360 games of chess at the same time over a period of 14 hours. He won 284 games—that's a 79 percent success rate—drew 70, and lost only 6.

Tall order

If Michael Jordan hadn't grown 4 inches in one summer he may never have been the basketball superstar he is! At high school, he was considered

TOO SHORT TO PLAY,

but a growth spurt set him on the path to stardom. He finished with an incredible career total of 32,292 points, the third highest in league history.

SNOW MAN

American Rainer Hertrich loves skiing so much that he's skied every single day since 2003! He has skied all over the world and once even trekked up an active volcano in Chile because it had more snow to ski down than neighboring mountains! His aim is to ski 100 million vertical feet.

WHAT'S YOUR GAMES?

So you're not the fastest athlete on the planet, but you might have won gold in some of the stranger events the Olympic Games have staged over the years...

Sailor's 100-meter freestyle
In 1896, only sailors in the Greek Royal Navy could enter, and there were only three competitors. So the winner was from... Greece!

Vertical rope climb
This was tricky, and, in 1896, only two of the climbers made it to the top of the 45-foot-long rope. After 1932 the event was no longer held.

Horses' long jump
First place at the Paris Olympics in 1900 went to Extra Dry, with a jump of 20 feet and a ¼ inch.

One-handed weight-lifting
The rules? Three lifts with each hand. The top three competitors then had three more turns to decide the winner.

Tug o' war
In 1908, the U.S.A. was beaten in just a few seconds by Great Britain. The losers accused team G.B., all policemen, of wearing illegal spiked boots, so there was a rematch, with G.B. in their socks! The U.S.A. still lost.

GRAVY FUN!

As much as 440 gallons of gravy were used in the World Gravy Wrestling Championships in Lancashire, England, in 2009. That's the equivalent of 40,000 portions! Sixteen competitors fought for the world title, which was won by Joel Hicks, a 30-year-old lawyer whose nickname is "Stone Cold Steve Bisto," who was watched by hundreds as he took the crown.

Honesty pays

While walking from school, some seventh graders found 66 tickets to a major league playoff game—worth

$20,000!

Instead of taking a few friends to the game, the boys turned the tickets in to the police who returned them to their owners—the Wachovia Bank. The boys were rewarded with luxury seats to a New Jersey Nets game, plus tickets to watch the Yankees.

At the end of a 2005 Namibian Cup soccer game in Africa, a penalty shoot-out went on for 48 kicks and lasted nearly an hour!

And the winner is...

Over five years, Swiss tennis player Roger Federer reached the semifinals or finals of more than 20 consecutive Grand Slam tournaments, and, from 2005 to 2007, he made it to ten

GRAND SLAM FINALS!

in a row. Between a loss at Wimbledon in 2002 and his defeat in the 2008 Wimbledon final, he won 65 grass matches in a row.

GOOD SPORTS...

Wrong field!

Cricketers in a game in India were astonished when a confused pilot landed a helicopter on their field during one of their games!

UHHHH!

Sister act

Venus Williams and her younger sister Serena are totally brilliant at tennis. Venus has 21 Grand Slam titles, Serena 27 of them! You wouldn't want to be dozing on the receiving end of Venus's serve—in Zurich in 2008 she hit the ball at 130 mph. It was the fastest women's serve ever recorded up to then.

Chain saws are hurled into the distance at the annual Chain-saw Chuck in Whitehorse, Alaska. Some chain saws have been thrown 55 feet!

Soccer run

In May 2009, at San Marcos, California, Abraham Munoz of the U.S.A. ran 1,000 meters in under 5 minutes, while keeping a soccer ball continuously in the air with his feet!

AWESOME!

Bass line

In the 25 years he's been fishing, Dave Romeo of Mount Joy Township, Pennsylvania, has caught more than 25,000 bass. A pretty remarkable achievement, but what's even more amazing is that he's kept a journal detailing every bass he's ever hooked!

How is the Central Asian sport of bazkashi played? Two teams of horsemen compete to grab an animal carcass and race it to their opponent's circle to score points.

That's cheating!

Can you believe that during the 1904 Tour de France—the world's most famous cycle race—French spectators were seen sprinkling nails and broken glass on the road, so that the leaders would get punctures and allow the local favorite to win?

Spun tale

The things people think of doing! New Yorker Ashrita Furman hula hooped underwater for 2 minutes 20 seconds at a dolphin center in Florida in 2007. He used a special metal hoop and was able to breathe air through scuba-diving equipment. "The dolphins thought I was totally crazy," he said.

TUMBLING TOWERS

If you visit the Tarragona Castells Festival in Spain, chances are you'll see lots of human towers, some of them standing solid and some in the process of

CRASHING DOWN!

Acrobats climb over each other to create these massive, dangerous towers, with as many as ten layers of people bravely standing on each other's shoulders.

Pound-out pounder

When boxer Eduard Paululum traveled to the Seoul Olympics in Korea, in 1988, he was the first ever Olympic competitor from the tiny Pacific island of Vanuatu. Unfortunately, he ate such a hearty breakfast before his weigh-in that he was disqualified for being 1 pound overweight and had to return home without competing!

During a 2008 Olympic pre-qualifying tournament, the Slovakian women's ice-hockey team scored at a rate, of more than one goal a minute, defeating Bulgaria 82 goals to 0.

In just one minute in Germany in 2007 Olga Berberich made 251 jumps with a skipping rope.

IN A WHIRL

American Bruce Crevier spun a single basketball on his fingers for over 22 hours. "I did eat and drink when I needed to," he admits, "and I also had to use the restroom on three occasions, but the basketball did not stop spinning." Using his hands, feet, knees, and even his mouth, American Bruce Crevier can also spin up to 21 basketballs all at the same time!

DON'T SING WITH YOUR MOUTH FULL!

Sam Simpson of Avalon, California, could hold either a baseball or three billiard balls in his mouth. It was a spectacular feat he demonstrated at the

1933 WORLD'S FAIR

in Chicago, Illinois. Not only that, but once his mouth was full, he could then burst into song to entertain the open-and-empty-mouthed spectators.

Paddling along

Organizers of the 2010 World Veteran Table Tennis Championships in Hohhot, China, were expecting some elderly players, but sprightly

100-YEAR-OLD

Dorothy de Low was a surprise! Known as "Dotty," she has been playing table tennis for 50 years and has won lots of of medals in seniors' competitions.

RIPLEY's ——

WAY COOL.

American skateboarder Danny Way is afraid of heights, but you'd never have guessed as he sped down a 75-foot-high ramp...

and leaped 70 feet through the air at a speed of...

50 MPH...

Welsh soccer fan Steve Thatcher named his son after all the players on his favorite soccer team, Cardiff City. It means Sam has 12 middle names!

Wobbly world

It's scary enough just standing on the edge of a volcano crater or on cliff tops, but Canada's Kris Holm rides around these crazy places on a unicycle! He's ridden on the rail of a 200-foot-high bridge, along the edge of a 2,640-foot-high cliff, and within 33 feet of red-hot bubbling lava on a volcano in Hawaii. He's one-wheeled across the Himalayan Kingdom of Bhutan and on the Great Wall of China, too.

... twisting and turning before landing a sensational backflip. He called the stunning maneuver El Camino ("The Way")...

and performed it in Mexico City in 2006, a year after he had jumped over the Great Wall of China!

UPS AND DOWNS

Fred Grzybowski of Los Angeles, California, can jump over a car on a pogo stick. The extreme pogo rider is able to bounce 8 feet into the air and can also perform an incredible nine consecutive pogo backflips. Pogo riders compete in a world championship called Pogopalooza, which attracts over 60 riders from the U.S.A, Canada, and the U.K. The best riders can perform more than

Eight boys aged between 8 and 11, jumping in shifts of two people at a time, bounced nonstop on a bouncy castle in Michigan for 24 hours in 2008.

220 BOUNCES IN A MINUTE!

BACKFLIP

8 FEET

Back in the U.S.S.R., during the 1930s, face-slapping was a recognized sport

SLEEPY HOT RODS

Every January, American bed-racing enthusiasts flock to Arizona for the annual Oatman Bed Race. Following a nightwear parade, teams of five people race beds down the main street at

BREAKNECK SPEEDS!

Then they make beds and race back to the finish line. Later in the afternoon, the same town comes together for a toilet-seat-tossing contest!

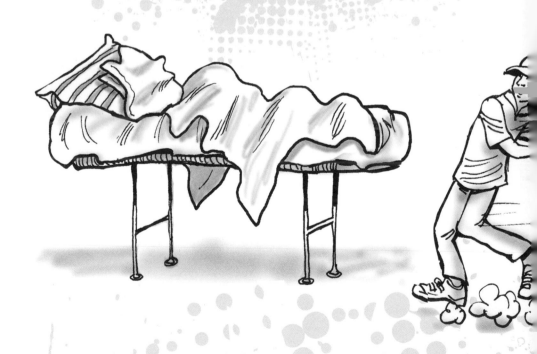

Sporty senior

Ray Moon of Victoria, Australia, started bodybuilding in 2004, age 75, and soon became one of the world's oldest competing bodybuilders. He won four state and national bodybuilding competitions by the time he hit 80! He training consisted of five fitness sessions a week, each including 2½ miles on a treadmill and 45 minutes of weights.

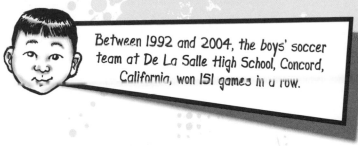

Between 1992 and 2004, the boys' soccer team at De La Salle High School, Concord, California, won 151 games in a row.

CRYSTAL CRAZE

A bike lock is a must on the low rider bike designed by the U.K.'s Ben Wilson, who brought a touch of bling to the humble bicycle by encrusting it with 110,000 Swarovski crystals! He was inspired by a visit to Hollywood, and the sparkly two-wheeler costs the grand sum of $50,000.

One hundred skiers traveled over 300 feet on a 100-foot-long pair of skis in Jacques Cartier Park, Ottawa, Ontario, in February 2005.

Weeeee!

David Kirke, founder of England's Dangerous Sports Club, adapted a medieval rock-throwing device called a trebuchet, so that humans could be catapulted

55 FEET INTO THE AIR

in under two seconds. The same club invented modern-day bungee jumping. Its fearless members have been known to hang-glide off active volcanoes and ski down artificial slopes balanced on a double-decker bus.

The odds of a baseball fan being hit by a ball during a Major League game are 300,000 to 1.

High drama

Wearing just the usual skimpy soccer shorts and shirts, players kicked off in freezing cold at a high-altitude

SOCCER MATCH

on June 8, 2007—at nearly 11,500 feet! The venue was Jungfrau Glacier in the European Alps, which is permanently covered in ice and snow. The air there is very thin, so players could manage to take part for only 10 minutes before becoming totally exhausted.

When basketball-mad Mike Campbell made 1,338 free throws in an hour—that's more than one every 3 seconds—over 90 percent of his shots hit the target.

Going nowhere fast

George Hood of Aurora, Illinois, rode a stationary bike for more than 176 hours over nine days in May 2008. He clocked up a mammoth 26,000 miles and burned nearly 47,000 calories, but saw nothing but the inside of one room.

FISHY TALE

Don't show up with a rod at the World Flounder Tramping Championships in Palnackie, Scotland—because contestants catch the fish with their bare feet! The rules are simple. At low tide, people wander over the mud flats of the estuary there and, when they feel the wiggle of a flat fish under their toes, they quickly trap it with their feet and pick it up! The person who catches the most fish is the winner.

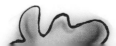

FUN AND GAMES...

Wee believe you

Most athletes turn to an ice pack to ease pain after an injury, but Ukranian heavyweight boxer Vitali Klitschko has a less appealing way to stop his fists swelling after a bout of fighting. He prefers to wrap his hands in his son's wet diapers, because, he says, baby urine is pure, doesn't contain toxins, and doesn't smell!

It took members of the Aurora Karate Club in Ontario, Canada, just 6 minutes 50 seconds to demolish an entire house.

Earth vs. astronaut

A team of U.S. students on Earth played chess against Canadian astronaut Greg Chamitoff in 2008—while he orbited the Earth in the International Space Station, traveling at 5 miles per second.

Swooping hawk

In 1999, Tony Hawk from San Diego, California, became the first skateboarder to land a 900—that's 2½ rotations in the air.

Ripley's——Believe It or Not!®

Pushy penguins

King and Gentoo penguins went beak to beak at the world's first sports tournament for penguins in Orakei, near Auckland, New Zealand, in May 2009. The so-called Penguathlon consisted of five nail-biting events—soccer, frisbee, surfing, swing ball, and waddle racing!

Upside-down descent

On December 28, 1949, gymnast Glenn Sundby became the first person to walk down the 898 steps of the Washington Monument on his hands.

Neck on the line

Fourteen-year-old sports fanatic Alfie Tyson-Brown of Dorset, England, played match after match for ten years, unaware that he had a broken neck, which could have killed him at any time. He played rugby, surfed, went mountain-biking, and rode roller coasters before he found out.

> When woodchopper James T Blackstone of Seattle went bowling, he scored 299.5 when one pin split in two and half of it remained standing!

RACE AGAINST TIME

Did you know that the modern marathon is named after the huge effort made by Pheidippides, a Greek soldier, in 490 BC? He ran from Athens to Sparta to ask for help in a battle; then back to Sparta; then on to Marathon to fight a battle; then back to Athens to announce that the Greeks had defeated the invading Persians. So, he ran over 300 miles in a week—that's 43 miles a day! The route was so exhausting that when he finally arrived in Athens, Pheidippides fell to the ground—stone dead.

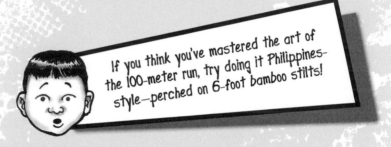

If you think you've mastered the art of the 100-meter run, try doing it Philippines-style—perched on 6-foot bamboo stilts!

High flyer

Not content with the thrill of a regular sky dive, Holly Budge from Bristol, England,

JUMPED FROM A PLANE

that was flying 29,000 feet over Everest, the world's highest mountain. During her descent to the Himalayas, she reached speeds of up to 140 mph and endured freezing temperatures of −40°F!

XXL TEE

A team from Bay College, Michigan, created a wooden golf tee that was over

26½ FEET TALL.

That's 80 times bigger than a normal tee! The head measured 35 inches in diameter, and the laser-cut, pinewood tee weighed in at almost a ton and took six months to make. So far, no caddy has come forward to offer to carry it!

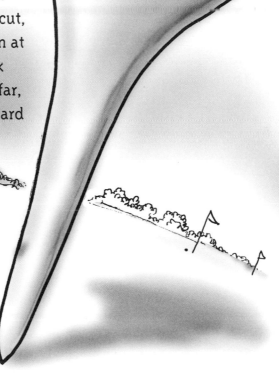

Time for a wash?

David Witthoft, a young Green Bay Packers' fan, was so excited by his 2003 Christmas gift—a Packers' jersey with Bret Favre's No. 4—that he wore it every day for over four years.

At the age of 67, Vijaypat Singhania flew a hot-air balloon to an amazing altitude of 68,986 feet over India.

RIPLEY's —◦ BEES 1, BASEBALL 0

① A 2009 baseball game between the San Diego Padres and the Houston Astros was in full swing...

② ...when it had to be abandoned at the top of the ninth inning. The reason? A swarm of bees!

The first ever car race was the 79 miles from Paris to Rouen in France in 1894. The average winning speed was just over 11 mph.

Built for speed

At the age of ten, Stephanie Beane of Grafton, Ohio, could roar around the track in a stock car at speeds of 80 mph! In her first race, she finished fifth in a field of 15, most of them adult men. She first got behind the wheel at two years old, and started racing at four. She was so successful that she began signing autographs at age six!

The bees had taken over part of the field at Petro Park, San Diego, California.

The players took flight, but not the bees, and fans had to be cleared out of several sections of the ground.

WATER WHEELS

You would think cycling underwater would be almost impossible! But, Maaruf Bitar of Lebanon loves it and he seems to be very successful at it. With an oxygen tank on his back, he practices his favorite hobby off the coast of the Mediterranean city of Sidon. Underwater cyclists have been known to ride at 200 feet below the surface of the sea. That's 30 times the depth of an Olympic swimming pool!

NUTTY PROCESS

Yak-skiing is catching on in Manali, India!

HERE'S HOW IT WORKS...

A person on skis stands at the foot of a hill holding a bucket of nuts. He is attached by a long rope—fed around a pulley—to a yak at the top of the hill. When the bucket is rattled loudly, the yak charges down the hill, pulling the skier up the slope. Easy!

While watching his favorite sport of football on TV, Elvis would wear a football helmet!

Brief encounter

On being presented with a gold medal at the 1956 Olympics, 18-year-old Russian Vyacheslav Ivanov decided to celebrate by throwing the medal in the air.

BAD MOVE!

His throw wasn't great and the precious award landed in a lake. Despite diving in to retrieve it, he never saw it again.

Big soccer matches often attract crowds of 70,000 people, but the 1950 World Cup final between Brazil and Uruguay was watched by nearly 200,000 spectators.

NO LIMITS...

Sports mad

John Carpenter of Firebrick, Kentucky, has collected 4,000 pieces of sports memorabilia, including autographed baseballs, basketballs, jerseys, helmets, and letters. Best of all, is the ball that famous baseballer player, Babe Ruth, hit for his 552nd career home run.

It took Ashrita Furman more than 12 hours to complete a 23-mile journey around New York City in 1997—by pogo stick!

High points

Maiko Kiesewetter of Germany was 13 years old when he scaled a 16-foot-high wall on a ladder of regular-sized playing darts in his hometown of Hamburg in November 2009.

Jack in the box

There are 92,542 seats at the Pasadena Rose Bowl stadium and, over a period of five days in 2008, Jim Purol of California sat in them all. He stood up and sat down for 12 hours a day, and took a cushion along to save getting a sore butt!

WOW!

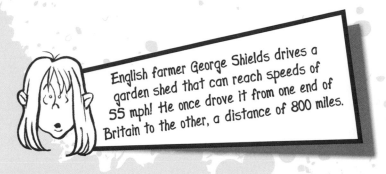

English farmer George Shields drives a garden shed that can reach speeds of 55 mph! He once drove it from one end of Britain to the other, a distance of 800 miles.

Hot trotters

Charloe Engle (U.S.A.), Ray Zahab (Canada), and Kevin Lin (Taiwan) ran the same distance as two marathons every day for 11 days to cross the 4,000-mile Sahara Desert on foot in 2007. They had to cope with temperatures that were over 100°F by day, but below freezing at night.

Out of sight

Minneapolis basketball star Wilfrid Hetzel shot 92 baskets out of 100 atttempts. That's amazing enough, but he was also blindfolded, used just one hand, and was standing on one leg!

Mister Plod

AWESOME!

Not surprisingly, the athlete wearing a 130-pound, old-fashioned, deep-sea diving suit at the 2003 Edinburgh marathon did not win—in fact he recorded the slowest time ever. Lloyd Scott, from London, crossed the line after 6 days, 4 hours, 30 minutes, and 56 seconds!

FLUSHED FACES

Some say you haven't lived until
you've had the pleasure of sitting on
a toilet seat in an outhouse on wheels
and been rushed through the streets of
Dawson City in Canada! In the Great Klondike

OUTHOUSE RACE

teams speed decorated outhouses—with topical
names such as The Elton John, The
Royal Flush, and The Whizzer of
Oz—around a 1½-mile course.
The rule is that one person
has to be sitting on the
toilet the whole time.

At just two years
old, Keith O'Dell
Jr. of Gloversville,
New York State, was
playing pool for up
to 3 hours a day.

In August 1983, a giant game of bingo was played at the Canadian National Exhibition with 15,756 people taking part!

Girl power

It's hard to believe now, but until 1928 women were not allowed to compete in any track and field events at the Olympic Games. In fact, some women collapsed at the end of the 800 meters in that year, so women were then banned from running races further than 200 meters until 1960!

HEAD LINER

Manoj Mishra of West Bengal, India, won a competition by balancing a soccer ball on his head for 14 hours. He wasn't allowed to touch it or move it during the competition, and he performed yoga to keep still during the attempt. Manoj perfected his skill while living on his own. "There was no one to play with, but I did not want to stop playing, so I used to practice juggling and balancing the ball," he said.

14.00

SNAIL'S PACE

Alain Jourdan, a French seaweed collector, is a champion snail-spitter. Yippee! He gained his title in August 2004, beating off 110 rivals from 14 different countries by

SPITTING A LIVE SNAIL

almost 31 feet from a running start. Despite winning, however, he failed to match his own record of just over 34 feet, because it was a windy day.

When table tennis was first played in England in the 1880s, it was played on a dining table, often using a cigar box as a paddle, books as a net, and a champagne cork for a ball.

THEY'RE OFF!

Ostrich racing is popular in Shanghai, China, where lightweight jockeys scoot about on the backs of the flightless birds at a speedy 45 mph. Ostriches are the fastest birds on the planet, and ostrich racing is taking off in South Africa and some parts of the U.S.A., too. But they're harder to steer than horses, and although jockeys wear saddles and reins, they still regularly fall off.

In the rough

You'll need brightly colored golf balls if you want to compete in the golf tournament at the Rein ski resort in Taufers, Italy. That's because it's played in up to 3 feet of snow, and at an altitude of 5,250 feet!

Michel Kapral from Toronto, Canada, ran a marathon in 3 hours 7 minutes in 2005, and did it while juggling three balls!

Altogether now

To celebrate the first anniversary of the Beijing Olympic Games, nearly

34,000 PEOPLE

gathered in the Chinese capital city in August 2009 and simultaneously performed the martial art of tai chi.

Ripley's Believe It or Not!®

Tries harder

Underwater rugby is a hit in Switzerland, where there are lots of teams. The six-a-side game is played by both men and women, who wear flippers, a snorkel, and goggles. The aim is to get a ball (filled with saltwater and weighing 13 pounds) in the opposing team's basket on the floor of a swimming pool. Players dive, pass, and tackle, but come to the surface to breathe.

The 1972 Bandama Car Rally in West Africa was so hard going that none of the 52 starters finished.

Crazy golf

David Ogron is one big speedy hitter of golf balls. With the help of ball setter Scott "Speedy" McKinney, who puts each ball on the tee, Ogron hit

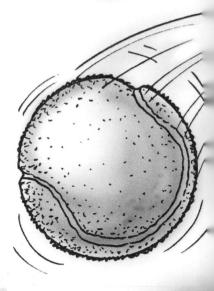

1,388 BALLS

in 30 minutes in May 2005 in Louisville, Kentucky. In July that year, he hit 82 in one minute. On another occasion, he hit 10,392 balls in 24 hours!

OUT!

Top tennis players Roger Federer and Andre Agassi may be high fliers in the tennis world but they took their game to a whole new level when they played high-rise tennis at a Dubai hotel. The court was marked out on the hotel's helipad, some 685 feet above the ground, with no fencing. If a ball sailed out, no one went to fetch it!

Ripley's
BOXING CLEVER

A former German riot police officer, Frank Stoldt, was crowned world champion of the hybrid sport of chessboxing in November 2007. Eleven rounds of chess then boxing are played, representing the ultimate test of brains and brawn. He fended off the punches of his U.S. opponent and then won the title with a checkmate in the seventh round.

Stop him!

Footballer Roy Riegels was famous for

RUNNING THE WRONG WAY

during a 1929 Rose Bowl game, while playing for the California Golden Bears. He picked up a fumbled ball and, losing his sense of direction, set off toward his own end zone. After running 70 yards, he was finally grabbed by one of his teammates on his own one-yard line.

In 1991, John Kockelman rose 5,000 feet in a hot-air balloon above California, and then made a 1000-foot bungee jump out of the basket.

Cry wolf

You should see the faces of beach-goers when a surfer walks out of the sea wearing a wetsuit by Dutch designer Diddo—especially the one that looks like the aftermath of a shark attack! Diddo doesn't like boring black wetsuits, and his other designs are just as bizarre, including a muscle model and a whale shark pattern!

TEENY-WEENY WHEELIE

Even toddlers would struggle to get their legs around
Bobby Hunt's special bike, as it's only 3 inches long,
and just 7¾ inches tall. Bobby spent more than $1,500
building and fixing the bike, so it's just as well that,
despite its tiny proportions, he can ride it—
and can even perform wheelies.

BALLED HEAD

In 1995, Zack Phillips of San Francisco invented the game of roller soccer, which is soccer on in-line skates. To promote the game, Phillips turned his head into a soccer ball, tattooing his scalp with hexagons, so he just had to dye the hair within the lines. He also dyed his eyebrows and beard to match. So, running his fingers through his hair could be considered handball!

EWE JOKING?

In which sport must competitors retire at the age of ten or under? "Mutton bustin," of course! Or, to give it its formal title, riding sheep rodeo style. At the 2006 Truckee Rodeo at Sierra, Nevada, Ryan Murphy won the title for the second successive year, but had to retire shortly afterward at the age of eight because he was about to exceed the riding weight limit of 60 pounds. The secret of his success was to sit on the sheep backward, and he managed to stay put for 22 seconds!

In Sibiu, Romania, in 2007, 24 people played basketball for 80 hours straight.

Leap of faith

It takes guts to trust a 500-year-old parachute. Yet that's just what Olivier Vietti-Teppa of Switzerland did when he made a

2,000-FOOT JUMP

from an airplane using a parachute based on the design of the artist and inventor, Leonardo da Vinci, drawn in 1485! Vietti-Teppa wore a reserve parachute, just in case da Vinci's didn't open, but it worked perfectly in the end, although it was impossible to steer.

WINNING STREAK...

Fast tracker

At the 2008 Beijing Olympics, Jamaican runner Usain Bolt won the 100 meters in a world-record smashing time of 9.69 seconds—even though he slowed down to celebrate and had his left shoe lace undone!

Everyone's awake at the Sheep Counting Championships of Australia, when several hundred sheep run across a field while competitors try to count them.

Billion-dollar man

Tiger Woods became the first-ever sportsman to earn a billion dollars. The U.S. golfer has won more than 70 tour events and, when he was only 3 years old, he shot an amazing score of 48 over nine holes at a golf club in California.

AMAZING!

Schoolboy error

In 1823, William Webb Ellis, a student at Rugby School, England, caught the ball during a game of soccer and ran to the opposing team's goal. It was the birth of rugby!

Tower of strength

If you take the elevator to the observation deck of the Empire State Building, you'll be there in less than a minute. But, every year, 300 runners take part in a race to the same spot, up the stairs—1,576 of them to be precise—passing 86 floors, and climbing to 1,050 feet. The sprint takes most of them about 15 minutes.

Over the course of 2,062 days between 1997 and 2003, Robert Garside from England ran 30,000 miles around the world.

Seasoned player

Only a few athletes have won medals at both the Summer and Winter Olympics. Canada's Clara Hughes is one of them, succeeding at both cycling and speed skating.

WOW!

Up to speed

Twelve-year-old Michael Hoffman, a taekwondo black belt from Ann Arbor, Michigan, managed to kick a cushioned pad 2,377 times in a single hour in October 2005. He alternated between his left leg and his right. Let's do the math—that's over 38 kicks a minute, or about one every 1.5 seconds!

AWESOME!

Ripley's
IT'S HAND MADE!

Most people have played Rock, Paper, Scissors at some time. Well, now everyone can go along to the RPS World Championships held in Toronto, Canada. Although, RPS was originally a children's game, there are now more than 2,200 members of the World Rock, Paper, Scissors Society and players travel to Toronto from all over the world. It's a serious business—the winner collects $7,000 in prize money.

Rock...

Paper...

Scissors...

Rich!

GREAT BALLS OF FIRE

Pelota is one of the world's oldest ball games—
it was first played 3,400 years ago. In October
2005, to celebrate this ancient sport, a museum
in Mexico City, Mexico, put on a
match in which the players whacked a

FLAMING RUBBERBALL

with hockey-style sticks. The burning ball
symbolized the sun, or a comet. In ancient
times, the result of a game of pelota often
helped to decide which of two courses of
action should be taken.

65

Marcus Stoeckl from Austria reached a speed of 130.7 mph in 2007, when he rode a mountain bike down a snow-covered mountain in Chile.

DOiNG THE ROUNDS

See if you can do this! Paul Blair from San Francisco, California, runs a mile in under eight minutes, while twirling a hula-hoop! Known as Dizzy Hips, Paul also hula-hoops while skating, skiing, or snowboarding. He can even use a giant hula-hoop that measures 43 feet in circumference.

In August 2009, Mike Filippone of New York swung at nearly 7,000 baseball pitches in just 13½ hours.

HIGH OLD TIME

There's just one main rule for a certain race in Nanning, Guangxi Province, China, but it's weird one—all runners have to wear high heels! Men have to wear shoes with a 3-inch heel, while women have to wear 4-inch stilettos because they are more used to wearing high heels than men!

PLAYING GAMES...

Ready to drop

Maybe they just didn't hear the whistle, but a 52-hour marathon basketball game was played at New England's Beatrice High School gym between July 28 and July 30, 2005. Apparently, it got tough at around 40 hours, when some players were begging to give up, but they all battled on. The final score was 7,935 points to 6,963.

AWESOME!

Peak fitness

In the Tour de France cycling race, a cyclist can burn up to 10,000 calories during a mountain-stage day—that's more than four times as much as someone walking for 75 minutes a day for an entire week.

The U.S.A. are the Olympic rugby champions. They beat France 17–3 in the final when rugby was last featured in the Olympics—in 1924!

Marathon man

Rikki Cunningham played 80 different opponents during his 72-hour, nonstop billiards stint in Greensboro, North Carolina, in August 2009.

WOW!

It took Englishman Martin Downs just eight days to skydive on six continents—Asia, Africa, Europe, South America, North America, and Australia.

Relative pain

At the World Indian-Eskimo Olympics, ear-pulling is a sporting event. String is stretched between the ears of two people until one person yells "uncle!"

UHHHH!

Costume drama

When a soccer team brings out a new team shirt, the supporters tend to wear it as well. So, the mind boggles over what might happen in Florence, Italy, when an annual soccer match called the Calcio is played between two teams of 27 players dressed in 16th-century costume! It's a rough game. Players are allowed to elbow, kick, and even head butt each other.

AMAZING!

Going for gold

New Zealanders compete annually to see who can throw a gumboot (a farmer's boot) the farthest. The winner receives the honor of a Golden Gumboot!

Caught in the act

Super-speedy juggler Zdenek Bradac from the Czech Republic, while juggling three balls, made 339 catches in just 60 seconds.

Still got bounce

Marques Haynes of the Harlem Globetrotters
played basketball for more than 50 years, making his
final appearance in 1997 when he was

IN HIS SEVENTIES!

He played more than 12,000 games in 97 countries,
and could dribble the ball six times a second, with his
hand just a few inches from the ground.

Brian Jahrsdoerfer, Michel Lavoie, Peter Okpokpo,
and Warner Tse played doubles tennis for
48 consecutive hours in Houston, Texas, in 2006.

High flier

Who in their right mind would drop head
first, from a height equivalent to a four-story
building—even if the landing is into
water? Yet that's just what Tom Daley does
almost every day. In 2009, aged just 15, he
became the world 10-meter platform diving
champion, and the youngest diver ever to win
a title in men's platform diving.

RUN FOR YOUR WIFE!

For the purposes of the Wife-carrying World Championships in Finland, it's a mixed blessing if a man's wife is on the large side. On the one hand, the husband will find running over the 832-foot-long obstacle course with his wife upside down over his shoulder, or on his back, a little on the hard side. On the plus side, the prize for the winning pair is the wife's weight in beer!

MONKEY STYLE

Sport is branching out—into extreme tree climbing. American Peter Jenkins and his friends climb trees and perform acrobatic stunts. These include balancing on the branches and running (yes, running) across the tops of the trees! They also tree surf, where they go high into the trees on a windy day and ride the branches like waves.

Warm-up time

Just when you're poised to break the record for the longest ice hockey game, the last thing you want is for the ice to melt! Yet that's what happened in Edmonton, Alberta, when a team slogged through 87 hours 10 minutes of play, only for the game to be abandoned due to a

SLUSHY RINK.

So, the existing record for the longest game still stands, at 130 hours 7 minutes.

Rick Sorensen finished 18 holes at Meadowbrook Golf Club, Minneapolis, in 86 strokes blindfolded.

Top athletes

High fives for the highest marathon in the world!
The starting line is at 17,000 feet near

MOUNT EVEREST

Base Camp in Nepal, and runners tackle rough mountain trails, ice, wind, and two grueling uphill sections before arriving down in the town of Namche Bazaar at 11,300 feet.

ROCK-A-BYE TENT

Who could sleep easy in the Portaledge, a small portable tent, suspended by only ropes attached to temporary anchor points that are jammed into rock cracks thousands of feet up cliff faces? Surprisingly, climbers say the tent is very stable—some people have been known even to light gas stoves inside—although they recommend remaining harnessed to the cliff face when asleep, to prevent

FALLING OUT OF BED!!!

It's just a game...

Some games are just plain vicious and the 17th-century sport of shin kicking is one of them. In Gloucestershire, England, competitors, wearing white shepherds' smocks, grasp each other by the shoulders and land blows on their opponent's shins. In olden days, people would harden their shins with hammer blows beforehand and wear iron-capped boots! Now, players stuff their trousers with straw and wear soft shoes.

The 1900 Olympics featured live clay pigeon shooting. Nearly 300 birds were killed. It was the only time in Olympic history that animals were deliberately injured.

In with a shout

Ever have the feeling that no one's listening to you? Maybe you should head along to the National Hollerin' Contest, held each year at Spivey's Corner, North Carolina. Contestants yell as loud as they can for 4 minutes. Hollerin' was a traditional method of long-distance communication before the invention of the telephone.

JUST POPPING OUT...

When Californian Andre Tolme visited Mongolia in 2001, he reckoned it was the world's most naturally formed golf course. So, he laid plans to play golf across the whole of the country—all 1,320 miles of it—avoiding, if he could, the world's largest bunker, Mongolia's Gobi Desert! Armed with 500 balls and two clubs, he teed off at Choybalsan near the Chinese border, aiming for the first hole "just" 138,889 yards due west.

...FOR A ROUND OF GOLF!

By August 10, 2003, he had completed nine holes in 5,854 shots, losing 353 balls along the way.

Speed merchant

Australian swimmer Ian Thorpe has won five Olympic golds and 11 World Championship golds, so it's no wonder he's nicknamed

"THORPEDO"!

What's weird is that as a child he was allergic to chlorine, so he didn't swim his first race until he was seven. Even then, his allergy forced him to swim awkwardly with his head out of the water. By 14, he was representing his country in tournaments.

Ripley's —— COLD CRICKET

Two teams of English cricketers trekked nine days to the slopes of Mount Everest in April 2009 to play a game of cricket at an altitude of 16,945 feet. The challenge was the brainchild of cricket enthusiast Richard Kirtley who had noticed that a plateau on the slopes of Everest looked just like a London cricket ground.

Bob Aube and Phil Marrone played golf for 500 miles from San Francisco to Los Angeles, taking 16 days and using 1,000 golf balls.

Game on... and on

Imagine the arm ache of Suresh Joachim who, in Toronto, Ontario, in June 2005,

BOWLED NONSTOP FOR 100 HOURS

—that's the equivalent of four whole days! He plowed on through 360 games of bowling in which he achieved a fantastic 120 strikes and broke nine bowling balls.

PLACE YOUR BETS

Believe it or not, camel racing is a serious sport in the Middle East and Australia, with big prize money and top camels selling for as much as $40,000. Jockeys have to keep their wits about them, as camels can run as fast as 40 mph in short sprints, and often suddenly stop mid-race and change direction without warning!

Lone ranger

Bob Holmes of Rumney, New Hampshire, has played almost

17,000 VOLLEYBALL GAMES

as a one-man team. He's beaten police departments, professional sports teams, and a team consisting of more than 1,000 people. In all, he has faced 400,000 opposing players, but has suffered fewer than 400 defeats, appearing in 5,500 gymnasiums in front of over 3½ million people.

In 2010, Tyler Toney, a student from Texas, made a basketball shot he threw from a low-flying airplane!

SPORTS CRAZY...

In 2005, Australian Matt Mingay performed a motorbike wheelie at a speed of 140 mph.

Given the slip

Riders race bicycles over a sheet ice course at the Montreal Ice Cup. How do they get a grip? By banging up to 400 screws into their rubber tires.

Too much yelling

Manchester United goalkeeper Alex Stepney dislocated his jaw while shouting at his team mates during a 1975 soccer match against fellow English club, Birmingham City.

Tummy ache

Fitness instructor Ken Richmond has stomach muscles like iron, and lets people fire cannon balls straight at them! Ok, so he staggers back a bit, but otherwise he suffers no ill effects. He can also survive having a cannonball dropped on his head and is able to withstand the force of a massive 4,000-pound wrecking ball slamming right into his abdomen.

WOW!

On a roll

Frenchman Jean-Yves Blondeau wears a special suit with wheels attached over his elbows, back, bottom, and knees. He rolls down the highway, in many positions, at up to 60 mph.

Lifting just one bowling ball is enough for most of us, but Bob Whitcomb, from Ohio, can juggle three, catching the 16-pound balls 82 consecutive times.

Fast track

You hear the screeching first, and then smell the burning rubber. Finally, in the motorsport of Gymkhana, you see the amazing driving skills. Drivers are required to drift sideways around seemingly impossible corners and spin through circles at breakneck speeds.

Ken Block is so expert at it that he can slide 360 degrees sideways around a moving target.

READY, STEADY, DUST!

Mark Tilbrook and James Doherty from the U.K., invented the silly sport of Urban Housework, which includes such skilled events as mop jousting in shopping carts, riding vacuum cleaners downhill, hoovering the great outdoors, and "apocalypse dishwashing!" Urban Housework is a similar group to the Extreme Ironing Bureau whose members iron in scary situations—on cliff edges, while scuba diving, or while bungee jumping. But don't ask either club to admire the bravery of the other—they are massive rivals!

ALL IN WHITE?

Bride-to-be Casey Squibb of Dorset, England, went bogsnorkeling on her bachelorette party and ended up recording the fastest time ever for a woman at the Irish Bogsnorkelling Championships in Castleblayney, Monaghan. Competitors have to complete two lengths of a 60-yard bog drain in the quickest time possible, wearing a snorkel, mask, and flippers. Casey added a white lace veil for the occasion.

GO GIRL!

Rally drivers

Twin brothers Ettore and Angelo Rossetti played a continuous tennis rally that lasted nearly 15 hours—with a total of 25,944 shots! The rally, played in August 2008, nearly came to an end hours earlier after 12,000 strokes, when Angelo tried to hit a shot while eating a PowerBar, but Ettore raced forward to save the day.

Richie Carrasco completed 142 nonstop, 360-degree spins on a skateboard in 2000.

Beginner's luck

Some golfers wait a whole lifetime for a hole in one, but in March 2009, Norwegian Unni Haskell hit just that with her first ever swing on a golf course. She'd had just two months of lessons before taking aim on the 100-yard hole in St. Petersburg, Florida. "I didn't know it was that big of a deal," she said. "I thought all golfers do this." Ugh!

READY, STEADY, SPIT!

Perhaps not a sport for the more genteel among us, cherry-pit spitting has become a popular event and people even compete at national and international competitions. At the 2006

WORLD CHAMPIONSHIP

in Germany, Franz-Wolfgang Coersten spat a pit an incredible 63 feet 4 inches—that's about two-thirds the length of a basketball court!

You're out!

In June 2009, an umpire at an Iowa high-school baseball game threw out the entire supporting crowd. Don Briggs took the drastic action during the game between Winfeld-Mount-Union and West Burlington because he said the fans were yelling and arguing.

At the Sheep Counting Championships of Australia, hundreds of sheep run across a field while competitors try to count them.

Ripley's LEAPS OF FAITH

In Valencia, Spain, the unusual sport of bull-leaping takes place in front of huge crowds. It's not a pastime for the faint-hearted! Bull-leapers carry on a tradition that goes right back to 1500 BC.

Bull-leapers face a bull as it charges and, at precisely the right moment...

ATTENTION SEEKER

Jessica Bruinsma from Colorado Springs, Colorado, was rescued from a German mountain in 2008 by sending an S.O.S. with her bra! She'd fallen into a crevasse and was stranded on a ledge at

4,000 FEET.

After three days, she alerted the attention of emergency services by hooking her brightly colored sports bra like a flag on a cable used to transport logs.

...they jump over the speeding horns—toes pointed, arms outstretched, maybe adding a somersault or a twist.

The leapers risk death or injury, but the bull always remains unharmed.

In September 2004, U.S.A.'s Andy Roddick hit a 155-mph serve—that's the same speed as an express train. "I hit a good one. That's about it," he said modestly.

Keep the ball rolling

Many of us like a game of softball, but how many would endure one that lasted 96 hours 4 minutes? That staggeringly long game was played in Charlottetown, Prince Edward Island, Canada, in 2008, by 40 players—male and female. There were 467 innings and 1,941 runs were scored.

Armenian gymnast Davit Fahradyan managed a mind-blowing 354 turns on a horizontal bar in Yerevan, Armenia, in July 2009.

JUMPING FOR JOY

Sebastien Foucan invented the extreme sport of free-running. It's a form of acrobatics, in which participants can scale buildings, run along narrow ledges, and jump from rooftop to rooftop. Foucan once performed a 20-foot jump from the bridge to a gun turret on a battleship! "It's a way of facing our fears and demons and you can apply this to the rest of your life," he says.

Gone with the wind

You'd think that there was enough time to make
a relaxed parachute landing after a

LEAP FROM A PLANE

at 18,000 feet, but when the aim is to get 108 jumpers
into formation during such a fall, time passes fast.
In the skies over Illinois in 2009, after freefalling
for 40 seconds at 180 mph, the 108 daredevils
got themselves into position and held on tight,
completing the formation for just a few seconds
before breaking apart for landing.

BOY WONDER

At just eight years old, Tiger Brewer from London, England, stood on the top of a biplane flown by his grandfather at 100 mph. His wing walking took place at a height of 1,000 feet above an airfield in England in August 2009. He was following a family tradition—Tiger's grandfather manages SuperAeroBatics, the world's only formation wing-walking team.

Andrea Holt played a nonstop single table-tennis rally with Alex Perry and Mark Roscaleer for 8 hours 27 minutes at Manchester, England, in 2007.

Donald "D.J." DeWoff has created a multicolored fence from more than 700 surfboards near his Hawaii home.

Name game

An Italian amateur soccer team drives referees mad because every single player has the same surname—De Feo. What's more, the coach, secretary, doctor, and all 12 sponsors of the club are also called De Feo—and the team's ground in Serino is located on Raffaele De Feo street.

95

Ripley's—Believe It or Not!®

Flavio Jardim and Diogo Guerreiro windsurfed along the entire coastline of Brazil, all 5,045 miles of it, between May 2004 and July 2005.

Every year, more than 400,000 people in the U.S.A. compete in marathons.

In 1931, the owner of the Chattanooga Lookouts baseball team traded player Johnny Jones to another team in exchange for a 25-pound turkey.

Pat Keller of North Carolina plunged down the 120-foot La Paz waterfall in Costa Rica in a kayak, at around 300 feet per minute.

In Puerto Rico, a racehorse called Camarero won 56 races in a row between 1953 and 1955.

Basketball star Riley McLincha of Clio, Michigan, can juggle and dribble three basketballs at the same time. That makes him a drubbler!